The

Credit
Repair

Answer
Book

The
Credit
Repair
Answer
Book

GUDRUN MARIA NICKEL
Attorney at Law

SPHINX® PUBLISHING
AN IMPRINT OF SOURCEBOOKS, INC.®
NAPERVILLE, ILLINOIS
www.SphinxLegal.com

First Edition: 2007

Published by: Sphinx® Publishing, An Imprint of Sourcebooks, Inc.®

Naperville Office
P.O. Box 4410
Naperville, Illinois 60567-4410
630-961-3900
Fax: 630-961-2168
www.sourcebooks.com
www.SphinxLegal.com

This publication is designed to provide accurate and authoritative information in regard to the subject matter covered. It is sold with the understanding that the publisher is not engaged in rendering legal, accounting, or other professional service. If legal advice or other expert assistance is required, the services of a competent professional person should be sought.

From a Declaration of Principles Jointly Adopted by a Committee of the
American Bar Association and a Committee of Publishers and Associations

This product is not a substitute for legal advice.

Disclaimer required by Texas statutes.

Library of Congress Cataloging-in-Publication Data
Nickel, Gudrun M.
  The credit repair answer book : immediate relief from your credit problems
/ by Gudrun Maria Nickel. -- 1st ed.
     p. cm.
  Includes index.
  ISBN-13: 978-1-57248-573-0 (pbk. : alk. paper)
  ISBN-10: 1-57248-573-6 (pbk. : alk. paper)
  1. Consumer credit--United States. 2. Finance, Personal--United States.
3. Credit ratings--United States. I. Title.

HG3756.U54N53 2006
332.7'43--dc22

2006031231

Printed and bound in the United States of America.
SB – 10 9 8 7 6 5 4 3 2 1

Contents

SECTION I: BUILDING GOOD CREDIT

Foreclosing a Deed of Trust
Selling the Property before Foreclosure
Deed in Lieu of Foreclosure
Negotiating with Your Lender
If You Are in the Military
Recap—Steps You Can Take after Foreclosure Is Started
For Further Research
Sample Mortgage Foreclosure Complaint
Responding to a Foreclosure Complaint
Sample Answer to Foreclosure Complaint

Personal Financial Assessment Chart
Monthly Expenses Chart
Assets Chart
Assets Given as Collateral Chart

Restrictions on Repossession
Sale of Collateral after Repossession
Lender's Pattern of Accepting Late Payments
Your Remedies
If the Lender Already Has the Collateral
Property Exempt from Creditors
For Further Research

Judgment
How a Creditor Gets a Judgment
Your Defenses to the Petition or Complaint
Moving to Another State
Confession of Judgment
Possible Alternatives if the Debt Is Legitimate
Effect of Judgment on Credit Report

SECTION III: PROTECTING YOUR FUTURE CREDIT

Introduction

Although the use of credit dates back several centuries, it is only in the past half century that the majority of people in the United States, in nearly every walk of life, use credit in one form or another. Credit, or borrowed money, is used to purchase a house, car, clothing, food, and entertainment. A credit card is necessary to make airline and hotel reservations, rent a vehicle, and connect to utilities. Although credit is a necessary part of our lives in today's world, it is not given to us automatically. We must first apply and be approved by the lender, whether it be a bank, credit card company, finance company, or retailer. Once approved, we must learn to use credit cautiously and responsibly. When we use credit, we create debt that must be repaid.

Occasionally our debt becomes overwhelming, resulting in a bad credit history, money judgments, and sometimes bankruptcy. In these cases, good credit must be reestablished.

Section I of this book explains how to first establish credit, reestablish credit, and maintain good credit. The first section, *Frequently Asked Questions*, answers common questions about credit and debt. Chapter 1 describes the nature and use of credit and its history. Chapter 2 provides an overview of the types of dept. Chapter 3 explains your credit report and what you can do to change it. Chapters 4 and 5 detail how to establish good credit and how to use credit responsibly.

Section II acknowledges that people do have financial difficulties; explains the types of debt, the lenders, and the obligations to give detailed and accurate information about the credit being extended; and, provides tools for dealing responsibly with creditors.

As stated in the June 16, 2006, issue of the *Financial Times*, "Middle America is flirting with a personal finance problem....The trail of this spend, spend culture is littered with personal bankruptcies."Although careless spending—particularly purchases on credit—is likely to result in unwanted consequences, even the most responsible and conscientious person can experience a change in economic circumstances that may be financially and psychologically devastating. Lifetime careers sometimes die an early death; if you become ill, there is often too little or no disability insurance. A job loss or illness can make it difficult, if not impossible, to meet your financial obligations. Lenders who were once pursuing you to lend you money will soon pursue you to get the money back if you fail to make the required payments.

The only way to avoid having creditors is to avoid having any debt. However, most people have a mortgage on their homes, have purchased one or several vehicles on credit, may have a consumer loan for household items, and have a number of credit cards. Your creditors— mortgage and finance companies, banks, credit card companies, etc.—all expect to get paid.

When you do not pay, your creditor has a number of options available in attempting to collect an outstanding debt. The creditor can:

- send your account to a collection agency. The agency rather than the creditor will then write and call you to try to collect the payment. (If the creditor assigns its right to the account, the collection agency can sue for the amount due in its own name.);
- report your unpaid bill directly to a credit reporting service (credit bureau), and then send it to a collection agency;
- get a judgment against you in court;
- foreclose on your real estate and get a deficiency judgment if the sale proceeds are not enough to cover the debt;
- repossess your personal property that is used as security for a loan, sell it, and get a deficiency judgment if the amount of the sale is not enough to cover the debt;

- get an assignment of property you are expecting to receive, such as a tax return or royalties;
- take your property, either before or after getting a judgment against you;
- garnish your wages; or,
- force you into bankruptcy.

Although most people do not openly discuss financial problems, they are a reality of life, particularly in an economy where thousands of people are being laid off or terminated from their jobs. Even if you are getting unemployment benefits, they may not be sufficient to meet the financial obligations you took on while earning a good wage or salary.

It is easy to become overwhelmed by the pressure of collectors' calls and a mailbox full of overdue bills. Being served with a summons in a lawsuit filed by a creditor to collect an unpaid debt—a good possibility if your bills are overdue—is an experience most people would rather live without.

Becoming overwhelmed or having anxiety attacks does not solve financial problems. In order to deal with financial setbacks effectively, it is important to have an understanding of what your rights are, the extent a creditor can actually go in collecting a debt, and how you can defend yourself against the actions your creditors might take to collect debts.

This book explains what types of actions creditors can take against you for nonpayment and your possible defenses to those actions.

The federal laws apply if:

- you enter into a written agreement with the creditor regarding the debt;
- the extension of credit is for personal, family, or household purposes;
- if the creditor (or collector) involved during the immediately preceding calendar year, entered into agreements with consumers involving interest or finance charges, or extensions of credit involving more than four installments more than twenty-five times; and,
- payments are to be made in more than four installments or interest is added that was not previously charged.

This book contains information about your rights under these federal laws regarding collection agencies, credit reporting, consumer loans, credit cards, and leases in Chapters 6, 7, 9, 10, 11, and 12.

An isolated transaction with someone to whom you owe money will probably not be regulated by federal law; however, there may be state laws for your protection. Chapters 15 and 16 deal with judgments and collections, and they will apply whether or not your loan or lease transaction is subject to federal law.

In a good economy, lenders readily give credit to most people—many lenders even have employees whose sole job is to find borrowers. In some cases, perhaps lenders were overly zealous in their efforts to extend credit to you, and now when times are tough, you may find it difficult to repay those obligations. There are numerous laws that have been enacted to protect borrowers from certain lender and creditor tactics, and you may find that you indeed have some recourse by reading this entire book.

Having a better understanding of the different types of debt you have incurred, and what your legal rights are in the event of your inability to repay a loan or credit obligation, will help you take control of whatever financial dilemma you may find. You should take some comfort in knowing that you can no longer be put into prison for being in debt based upon any type of contractual obligation to pay.

Being in overwhelming debt should be viewed as a temporary condition—in which you may find yourself due to present circumstances. It is a condition that can be changed, through your own efforts in dealing with creditors or perhaps ultimately filing a bankruptcy petition.

Chapter 17 gives you bankruptcy information. The most important point to keep in mind is that all hope is not lost. Chapter 19 explains how to reestablish credit after financial difficulties, including bankruptcy filings. Chapter 20 helps you better protect yourself from financial problems in the future.

Some chapters include a section on how to exercise your rights or defenses with some sample letters and forms. You should use these with other resources available to you, including your local law library (often your local library will have books that contain your state as well as federal laws), your state or district attorney's office, your local court clerk, and your state or local consumer affairs or public service office. The state offices are listed at the back of this book in Appendix A.

For your convenience and for further research, the sources of information are listed at the end of each chapter. The numerous websites found in this book provide a wealth of valuable information about obtaining and maintaining good credit, and your rights as a consumer and debtor under the various federal and state laws. Information about credit and your rights as a consumer is available from:

Federal Citizen Information Center
Pueblo, CO 81009
888-878-3256
www.pueblo.gsa.gov

You will find that the terms *lender* and *creditor* are used repeatedly. Although there may be a technical difference in that a lender is in the business of lending money, while a creditor is in the business of extending credit (such as a credit card company), the terms are used interchangeably.

Frequently Asked Questions

Q
Why do I need credit?

A
While few of us are fortunate enough to have inherited enough money to pay cash for a house or car, most of us will need a loan to make major purchases. Many students need financial aid for college. Also, credit cards are required for hotel and airline reservations, car rentals, and Internet purchases. *Credit*, in this case, refers to an amount of money at your disposal for a variety of purposes.

Q
What is the difference between a credit card and a loan?

A
The result of using either is the same—money that was loaned for a purchase or some other purpose (such as education) must be repaid. A credit card is typically considered an *open-end* loan, similar to an *equity line of credit* with a maximum amount from which you can borrow.

A credit card is, in reality, a loan from a lending institution that pays the merchant to whom you gave your card number within a few days of receiving the credit card receipt. Repeated transactions are anticipated at a prescribed finance charge to be assessed on the unpaid balance.

On the other hand, a loan from a bank is often for a specific amount that is given to the borrower (debtor) at a specified interest rate with pre-determined payments. (There are many variations, however.)

Q
What if I have never had a loan before?

A
Your first step should be opening a savings and checking account. Once you have accumulated several hundred dollars, ask the bank for a *secured credit card.* Your deposit will be used as security for payment in case you default. You may also try getting your first loan with a *cosigner,* often a parent. Anyone to whom you have owed and repaid a debt can be a good reference when applying for credit.

Q
What is the difference between a credit card and a debit card?

A
A credit card is, in reality, a loan; you will need to pay back the principal plus all accrued interest according to the terms to which you have agreed. A debit card is similar to a check; the payment is immediately deducted from your account.

Q
How do I apply for a loan or credit card?

A
An application form must be completed; the amount of information required depends upon the lender. Questions include your name, address, social security number, name and address of employer, how long

you have been employed there, whether you rent or own your home, and your annual income. All information you provide must be accurate, so there won't be any discrepancies.

Q
Where can I find the terms of the loan?

A

The federal *Consumer Credit Act* requires disclosure by lenders of the total cost of credit, the amount and due dates for repayment of the loan, the amount of any late payment fee, etc. The credit card companies provide a detailed description of the terms and conditions that you should read and understand before accepting the card. Banks and other lenders provide the information in their *Truth-in-Lending* disclosure forms and other loan documents. These should be reviewed carefully and understood before signing.

Q
What is a credit bureau or credit reporting agency?

A

A *credit bureau* or *credit reporting agency* is a service that provides prospective creditors with the information about you: primarily the debts that you have and your payment record. The bank will request a credit report if you apply for a loan to buy a house. This report will tell the bank how many credit cards and other loans you have, whether or not you make your payments on time, whether someone has sued you and obtained a money judgment, and whether you have filed bankruptcy within the last seven years. There are three major credit reporting agencies in the country, namely Equifax, Experian, and TransUnion.

Q

What information does my credit report contain?

A

Your credit report contains your credit history, including: the names of all of your current and past creditors, your payment record, your employer's name and address, your employment history, current and previous addresses, public information such as judgments and bankruptcies, and any referrals by creditors to collection agencies.

Q

If a creditor reports my late payments to a credit bureau, even though I am doing the best that I can, what should I do?

A

You usually find out that a creditor has reported this type of information when you apply for a loan. If you are turned down for the loan because of your credit report, you have a right to a copy of the report free of charge. You are also entitled to one free copy per year of your credit report from each of the big three credit reporting agencies. (Go to **www.annual creditreport.com** for more information.) Otherwise, you can request a copy of your report from any of the credit bureaus, typically for a small fee. If there are negative notations on the report, write a letter to the credit bureau explaining the reason for the late or lower payments, and ask that a copy be given to anyone who requests a report. Before you apply for credit, you should make the prospective creditor aware of your situation so that there are no surprises for either the creditor or you.

Q

How does a lender decide whether I qualify for a loan or credit card?

A

First, your application is reviewed and information verified. A copy of your credit report is ordered and your credit history reviewed. Your total monthly obligations are considered in determining whether you can reasonably take on more debt; the length of employment may be considered in determining whether your income is stable enough to justify a loan. Some lenders also use a system called credit scoring to determine whether you are a good credit risk.

Q

What is a *credit score*?

A

A credit score is a type of grade given by a lender based upon your application and credit history, including the number and types of accounts, total outstanding debt, number of late payments, how long you've had your accounts, etc. The information is summarized to create a *profile*, which is then compared to others with similar profiles who have already been extended credit. The scoring system gives points for each item, which indicates that you are likely to repay the debt.

Q

Even though I have a fixed income, I get applications for credit cards in the mail. What should I do with them?

A

First, decide whether it is important or necessary that you have a credit card. Second, ask yourself whether you will use it responsibly. If the answers are yes to both questions, then:

- check the interest rate the credit card company is charging; whether it is only an introductory low rate or if it will go up; and, compare the rate with other companies;
- be sure you understand the repayment terms; whether you can pay the balance in monthly payments or whether the entire balance must be paid off monthly (for example, American Express cards require the entire balance be paid in full every month); and,
- check whether you will be charged an annual fee to use the card — try to find a credit card company that does not charge an annual fee.

Q
I've heard bankruptcy referred to as a quick fix for credit problems. Is bankruptcy really a way out of debt?

A
Bankruptcy should be used only as a last resort. For example, someone who has only one debt that cannot be paid in time should consider alternatives, such as working out a more reasonable repayment plan with the creditor, selling something to pay the debt, trying to negotiate a lower amount, or temporarily taking on a second job. Although bankruptcy may seem like an easy solution, remember that it will stay on your credit record for at least seven years and in the meantime you may find it extremely difficult, if not impossible, to get a mortgage or buy a new car. If a major catastrophe really does strike within that seven-year period, you will not be able to file for bankruptcy again.

Plus, under the new bankruptcy laws, more people are required to use a wage earners plan when filing for bankruptcy, which requires that you pay each of your creditors back over a period of time at a reduced amount. The plan must be approved by the bankruptcy court.

Q

If I do file for bankruptcy, is there any property I can keep for myself, or must all of my property be sold to pay my creditors?

A

Certain property is considered exempt from bankruptcy. In most cases you may keep your home (up to a specific dollar value) and some items of personal property.

Q

Will I still owe money after I file for bankruptcy, or will bankruptcy wipe out all of my debts so that I can make a fresh start?

A

It depends upon the debt. If you went on a major shopping spree, took a luxury vacation, and spent thousands of dollars using your credit cards, your creditors may convince the bankruptcy court that you should not be released from your obligation to repay the money. Bankruptcy will not eliminate most tax obligations (due for the three years immediately before filing), particularly not Social Security or withholding payments that you as an employer should have made for your employees. (Also, bankruptcy will not eliminate child support and alimony obligations.)

Q

Can I apply for credit after my debts have been discharged in a bankruptcy proceeding?

A

Certainly one can and should begin reestablishing good credit after bankruptcy. While some people report that they receive credit card applications in the mail immediately after their debts have been discharged, many find that reestablishing good credit takes some effort. The same steps should be taken as when first applying for credit—start with a secured card, cosigner, or perhaps a landlord who can verify consistent and timely payments. Local merchants who understand the reason for the bankruptcy — perhaps overwhelming medical bills — may be willing to extend credit.

Q
Can I pay more than the monthly amount due on the credit card statement or loan?

A
Not only is it possible, it is wise and responsible to pay as much as possible to reduce the outstanding loan balance, particularly on credit cards. Making only the minimum monthly payment, particularly on large balances, results in substantial finance charges. (For example, a $1,000 outstanding balance at 17.5% interest and repaid at $25 per month, will take over five years to pay and cost over $500 in total interest charges — more than half of the original principal balance.)

Q
Will I know when I am in financial trouble?

A
There are several signs that you may need help with your finances, including:
- juggling your bills from paycheck to paycheck and not being able to pay them all at one time;
- getting late payment reminders in the mail from your creditors; or,
- getting telephone calls from bill collectors. (This usually means that the person or company you originally owed money to has given up trying to collect the debt and has turned the account over to a collection agency.)

NOTE: *Most people in this country are in debt – debt includes the mortgage on your house, car and boat loans, loans to buy appliances and furniture, as well as medical and other bills.*

Q
How do people get into financial trouble?

A
Of course, we have all heard the story about the family who accepts every credit card that is offered by mail, then charges each card up to the maximum limit and cannot make the payments. Or, they can make just the bare minimum payment, which means that the outstanding balance, with accrued interest, may take an eternity to pay off. This problem stems in part from irresponsible use of credit, as well as eager credit card companies.

However, there are also many people who suffer catastrophies for which they simply are not prepared. For example, a medical emergency without proper insurance, or a job layoff, can have serious financial consequences for a family.

Q
Do I really have legal rights if I owe money?

A
Many people are surprised that there are laws, both state and federal, that protect them. For example, federal laws under the *Consumer Credit Act* include the *Fair Debt Collection Practices Act*, which protects you from being threatened by collection agency employees. Also under the *Consumer Credit Act*, the *Fair Credit Reporting Act* regulates credit reporting agencies and allows you to file a complaint with the government.

(For example, there are laws requiring auto leasing companies to give you certain information before you sign loan documents, as well as laws requiring auto leasing companies to give you certain information about the lease. There are also laws giving you an opportunity to tell your side of the story if the bank wants to foreclose your mortgage and take your house. In the end, if you find that bankruptcy is your only option, there are laws that will protect you and allow you to keep certain property. Of course, in order to use these laws to your advantage, you must know how they protect you and what action you need to take to protect yourself.)

Q
What can we do to prepare for an expected loss of income that will make it difficult, if not impossible, to pay bills?

A
The first step is to notify all of your creditors that you are having financial difficulties; and, in some cases, it may help to explain why. Ask the creditors if they will work with you on a reduced payment plan, perhaps giving you a few months of breathing room. Ask your home mortgage company if you could make interest-only payments for a period of time (provided these payments would be substantially less than the total) or a reduced payment with any unpaid interest to be added to the later payments after you get back on stronger financial feet. Be sure to ask your creditors if they will agree not to report your reduced payments to the credit bureau, as long as you keep your part of the agreement.

Q
I have a mortgage on my house, car payments, payments on some living room furniture, and several credit card bills. Is there a difference between these loans?

A
The mortgage on your house and the loan on your car are probably secured debts. In other words, the bank or creditors that loaned you the money to buy the house and the car have a legal interest in that property. It is referred to as collateral. If you do not pay, they have the right to take your property. This usually involves a court proceeding.

The other type of loan is unsecured. This means that the creditor has no collateral. However, the creditor can still sue in court, get a judgment against you, and then try to take your property or take the money from your paycheck to pay the debt.

Q

What if my ex-spouse and I agree to split the debts and my ex-spouse refuses to pay? A hospital where he had some surgery done keeps sending me threatening letters, but he agreed to pay the bill!

A

Unless the creditor, in this case the hospital, agrees in writing that it will look only to your ex-spouse for payment, your original agreement with the creditor still stands. In other words, the hospital is not a party to the agreement between you and your ex-spouse. If your ex-spouse does not pay, that leaves you responsible. (You can sue your ex-spouse for not living up to his or her part of the agreement.)

Q

Is it true that if I make a payment of $1.00 per month on a bill, I cannot be sued by the creditor?

A

This is a misconception that is absolutely wrong. If you owe an individual or a company money, that creditor has the right to get paid the full amount that is due, unless, of course, there is a valid legal defense to the bill. The defenses, that is, your possible legal and acceptable reasons for a nonpayment, are explained in detail in this book. However, making a payment of $1.00 per month is not a valid defense.

Q

What can I do if information on my credit report is wrong? For example, if there is an unpaid doctor bill on the report, to a doctor I do not even know? (Or if a bank loan that was paid off six months ago shows up as unpaid?)

A

The first step is to notify the credit reporting service, in writing, of the error. Be sure to send all letters certified, with a return receipt requested. If you are not sure how this is done, take your letter to the post office and tell the clerk that you want the addressee to sign a receipt for the letter. The clerk will give you the forms to complete. Once you have the receipt, the credit reporting service cannot claim that it did not receive your letter. The letter should clearly state which entry in the report is incorrect, and why. The reporting agency must investigate and correct the report if the information is found to be inaccurate. If the agency does not do what is required by law, you can file a complaint with the Federal Trade Commission.

Q

If all of my efforts to negotiate a reduced payment plan with a creditor fail, and the creditor does get a court judgment against me, how long will it stay on my record?

A

The credit report agencies will keep the judgment on your report for a period of seven years, unless the law in your state allows for a longer period of time, or the law allows the creditor to periodically renew the judgment. In some states, the judgment can stay on your report for as long as twenty-one years. This may make it difficult for you to buy a house or make other purchases on credit in the future.

Q

I have been receiving a lot of advertisements from companies promising to repair my bad credit. Are these legitimate?

A

You cannot change your credit history; no amount of money paid to a credit repair company will eliminate the fact that you owe money or failed to make payments in the past. The best credit fix is a disciplined budget and an effort to negotiate with and pay off your outstanding debts. The credit repair service (which will undoubtedly charge you a fee) may become another creditor.

Q

Several months ago I was having difficulty paying some of my bills because my hours at work were cut back, and I received letters from a collection agency threatening me with a lawsuit if I did not pay. Can you explain what a collection agency is?

A

A collection agency is a business that earns money by collecting debts for other people. For example, if you owe money to a doctor, and you are unable to work out a payment plan directly with the doctor's office, that doctor's office might turn the bill over to a collection agency. The collection agency usually gets a percentage of the amount it collects, and the balance goes to the creditor.

Q

Is there anything I can do to keep the debt collectors from calling at odd hours to collect a payment that I do not feel I owe?

A

The *Fair Debt Collection Practices Act* clearly states during what hours a collector may call you (8 a.m. to 9 p.m.). You should first tell the collector that you are aware of your rights under the Act, and that you will file a complaint with the Federal Trade Commission if he or she does not stop.

As soon as you receive your written notice from the collector, you should respond by certified mail, return receipt requested, explaining why you dispute the debt. The collector should not contact you again, but may pursue whatever legal remedies are available to collect payment. If a lawsuit is filed, you may then give your side of the story to the court. (You might also attempt contacting the creditor directly.)

Q

A good friend is having a difficult time buying a car because in the past he was late on a few bills. This shows up on his credit report and now he cannot qualify for a loan. His banker told him that the bank would give him a loan if he has a cosigner. My friend then asked me if would cosign his loan for him. Can you explain what this means to me?

A

Being a cosigner on a loan makes you as responsible for repayment as your friend. If your friend does not make the payments or is late for any reason, the bank can immediately try to get the money from you. Parents often cosign for loans for their children, since the children usually have not established a good credit report by the time they get their first car. In your case, however, you probably will not have as much control over whether your friend honors his obligation to the bank as most parents have over their children. Also remember that if your friend defaults and you are unable to pay the bank back, your credit report will also suffer.

Q

I am thinking about going into business for myself and will need to rent office space and lease some office equipment. Although I have already formed a company, the landlord and the leasing service insist that I personally guarantee the rental agreement. I thought that if I have a company, only the company should sign — is this not correct?

A

The landlord and equipment leasing company want to make sure that they get their money, even if your business fails. Your personal guarantee gives them the right to hold you personally responsible if your company cannot pay its bills. When you are personally responsible for the payments, your personal property, except, of course, the property that is exempt from creditors as explained later in this book, can be taken by the landlord or the leasing company. Usually this requires that the landlord or equipment leasing company go to court and get a judgment against you first.

Q

Please describe how a creditor can take my property if I have not given the creditor a security interest.

A

This is more easily explained by example. If you owe any money and do not make the payment when it is due, the person or company to whom you owe the money can file a lawsuit against you in court. If the judge decides against you, a judgment will be entered in the court records. The creditor can then take the next step and ask the court to *attach* (or take) certain items of your property in payment of the debt. If the court agrees, then the sheriff will be given the authority to take the property, sell it, use the money from the sale to pay the creditor, and any remaining amount will be paid to you.

Q

What does it mean to have your wages garnished?

A

This is a legal term which means that, after a creditor gets a judgment against you, the creditor can then ask the court to issue a garnishment. In other words, a court order will be sent to your employer demanding that a certain portion of your paycheck be withheld from you and sent directly to the court for payment to the creditor. Every time your paycheck is garnished, you will be getting a smaller amount than usual, and your creditor will be getting a portion of the money you owe.

Q

I have heard about mortgage foreclosures, but I am not sure how they work. Is this something only banks can do?

A

When you give a lender—regardless of whether the lender is a bank, the previous owner of the property, or your father—a security interest in your property (property here is real estate such as land, a house, or condominium), the lender has a right to take the property if you do not make the payments.

If your lender is threatening to foreclose its mortgage and take your property, be sure to read your mortgage very carefully to see if the lender is required to drop the foreclosure if you can come up with all the back payments due.

If it is impossible for you to make the outstanding payments, try to negotiate with the lender to take a *deed in lieu of foreclosure*. You would be transferring your ownership to the lender and avoiding the court procedure and possibly another negative entry on your credit report. Another option is to sell the property as quickly as possible, perhaps at a reduced price, and pay off the lender immediately to avoid court or foreclosure proceedings.

Q

The bank that gave us the money to buy our house required that we sign a stack of papers at closing, some of which I did not even have time to read or understand. Are there laws that protect people like me?

A

The *Consumer Credit Act* specifically requires that creditors provide you with certain information *before* you sign up for a loan so that you know exactly what your obligations will be, how much your payments will be, and the total amount the loan will cost you. If you have a thirty-year mortgage, you should know how much you will pay the bank if you make each and every payment for thirty years. The bank should also let you know what your closing costs will be. Often there are points, an origination fee, and other expenses that you will be required to pay for the privilege of borrowing money. These amounts must all be disclosed to you *before* you sign and commit yourself to the loan.

Q

I have often heard the phrase "don't mess with the IRS." Is there anything that can be done if I owe the IRS money?

A

First, do not assume that the IRS is always correct. However, always respond to any IRS notice within the time allowed to avoid any additional penalties and interest over and above the taxes you may owe. Be sure to keep all records—including copies of checks, receipts, and invoices—in case you are audited. The normal time limitation for an audit is three years, provided there was no fraud or gross misrepresentation of income. If you disagree with an IRS decision, you can file a petition in the U.S. Tax Court. If you have a serious problem or are in a crisis situation—such as job loss or medical emergency, the *Taxpayer's Bill of Rights* does require that an IRS officer—a Problem Resolution Officer—work with you to resolve the crisis.

BUILDING GOOD CREDIT

Chapter 1

Credit: A Vital Part of Our Economy

The use of credit certainly is not new or unique to the United States. It dates back approximately three thousand years. Legal documents such as bills of exchange and bank notes were used more recently, and items were offered for sale on credit terms as early as the 1700s. Credit is and always has been a vital part of our U.S. economic structure. Trade, national and international, is credit-based.

Letters of credit are used in business transactions, assuring a seller that the funds for a purchase will be available to the buyer. Farmers have relied on credit to keep their operations going, pledging proceeds from crops as payment for loans. *Credit*, even in the form of a credit card, is a loan that you are required to repay according to the lender's terms. A *lender*, in exchange for a fee (including interest), is advancing money to the borrower.

Credit also provides a significant income to many businesses and lending institutions. For example, a tire company might offer a payment plan to a buyer of a set of new tires. This plan is actually a loan to the buyer, requiring a specific amount to be paid every month. The payment amount typically includes interest at a predetermined rate. In this case, the tire company not only makes its profit on the retail sale of tires, but also on the monthly interest being paid on the loan. Most major retail stores offer their own credit cards or *loans* that increase the stores' total earnings. Many nonprofit organizations also offer their own credit cards in conjunction with a particular bank or credit card company, providing the organizations another source of funding.

Establishing good credit is a prerequisite for carrying on our daily lives. While we could argue whether credit is a good or bad idea, it seems that the vast majority of people need to use credit at one time or another. Not only is a good credit history required for major purchases, such as house and vehicle, other transactions can also involve a review of your *credit report*. For example, prospective landlords and employers may access your credit history. Condominium associations, as part of the new owner review and approval process, may require review of your credit report; applicants run the risk of being denied membership because of a bad credit history.

It is nearly impossible to rent a vehicle, make an airline reservation, reserve a hotel room, or establish utility accounts without a credit card number. Emergencies arise that necessitate the use of credit. Whether or not we like it, credit is a part of our daily lives. Our credit histories — those to whom we have owed money and our payment records — are now used as a measure of our fitness for a variety of purposes.

Chapter 2

Types of Debt—An Overview

Simply put, debt is owing money to someone else. However, there are many types of debt—each with its own legal and financial obligations. Understanding the various categories and types of loans available will strengthen your ability to better manage your own personal debt.

Secured Debt

All debts are either secured or unsecured. When an interest in property is given to your lender to make the loan safe, you have a *secured* debt. Examples of secured debt are your home mortgage and your car loan. The lender puts everyone on notice about its interest in your property by filing a mortgage on your real estate or a *security* interest in your personal property in the appropriate county or state records. The lender will secure its interest in a car or mobile home by placing its lien directly on the title.

When the lender has taken the proper steps to record its interest, you cannot sell the property without either paying off the lender or having the buyer take the property subject to the lender's interest. The property given as security is also referred to as *collateral*.

The lender may also take an interest in personal property by taking possession of it.

> **Example:** If you have given the lender stocks and bonds as collateral for your loan, the lender may hold these until the loan is paid

off, prohibiting you from using the same stocks and bonds as collateral for other loans or selling them.

Unsecured Debt Becoming Secured Debt

An *unsecured debt* may become a secured debt if a judgment becomes a *lien* (or claim) on your property. Even without judgments, some states allow liens to be filed. In Florida, for example, condominium associations generally have the right, without first getting a judgment, to place a lien on your property if you do not pay your condominium association assessments. Likewise, people you employ to work on your property or provide material may be able to file a lien before getting a judgment if you do not pay them.

A judgment may also become a lien on your property. Ultimately, the lienholder may take the property and foreclose its lien, just like a creditor to whom you actually gave a security interest in your property. (see Chapters 15 and 16.)

Selling Secured Property

If liens are not paid when you sell your property, they are not removed even if you transfer title. You may have considered selling to get out from under a mortgage obligation. However, a sale of property given as security will not necessarily relieve you of your responsibility to pay the mortgage holder, unless he or she agrees to let you off the hook and let your buyer take over the payments.

If you do not make the loan payments, the lender may, by proper legal proceedings and as specifically spelled out in the loan documents, take the property you have given as collateral. If the other lienholders are not paid when you sell, they can *foreclose* against you and the new title holder. (As for stocks, bonds, and items that the lender can hold in its possession, the lender can then sell them to pay off the debt.)

Lender Selling the Collateral

After the lender sells the collateral, depending upon your loan agreement, he or she will then apply the money from the sale, less expenses, to your loan. This does not necessarily mean that you are no longer liable to your lender. The loan document you signed may also give the lender the right to get a deficiency judgment against you if the amount realized from the sale is not enough to pay the balance due on the loan. (Deficiency judgments are discussed in other chapters in this book.)

Right of Set-Off

If you have several accounts at one bank as well as a loan, and you fail to make your payments on the loan, the lender may have the right to take the money from your deposit accounts and apply it to your debt. This is called the bank's *right of set-off*.

However, the bank may do this only if this was disclosed to you in the loan documents. The bank cannot use your other accounts as collateral without meeting the disclosure requirement. Otherwise, you can sue the bank for damages, including any cost to you for overdrawn checks. (If the bank has issued you a credit card, it is prohibited from taking funds from other accounts to pay any outstanding amount on the card.) (see Chapter 10.)

Bank's Tools

Bad debt has been a problem for banks for a long time. When a customer failed to make a payment within fifteen days of the due date, a late payment letter was sent. The letter was then followed up by a telephone call if no payment was received within thirty days of the due date.

With updated technology, however, a bank or lender can now target individual customers with tailor-made collection techniques. The customer's personal information is reviewed, along with credit reports and other financial information. The combination of information allows the bank or lender to plan its collection efforts on an individual basis. The information also helps the bank or lender decide whether to assign a case to a collection agency, and even suggests how the collection agency should handle the case.

New computer software helps lenders predict which cases are likely to end in repossession of the property, and puts the lender on notice to act immediately when a payment is late.

Unsecured Debt

An *unsecured loan* is one for which the lender has taken no collateral. Most credit cards and any loan given to you requiring only your signature are *unsecured loans*. (The signature of someone guaranteeing payment, or a cosigner, is given as security for the debt.) Unsecured debt also includes any amount you owe for services, such as doctors' bills. The service provider (i.e. hospital, doctor, dentist, accountant) and the creditor of an unsecured debt will often first try to contact you personally in an attempt to work out payment of the outstanding bill.

Debt after a Divorce

Marriage, divorce, and debt are discussed in detail in Chapter 18. Anyone who is contemplating separation or divorce should keep in mind that an agreement between you and your spouse is effective only between the two of you. Unless a creditor agrees in writing to release one or the other, both parties remain fully responsible for payment.

Contingent Liabilities

If you have a *contingent liability*, you will be liable for payment to a creditor only in the event the primary borrower does not pay.

> **Example:** If you have personally guaranteed payment of a business loan and the business can no longer make the payments, the creditor will look to you for the balance owed. Likewise, if you cosign on a loan for your daughter to buy a car, and she stops making the payments, the lender will come to you. You may be held responsible and pursued by the creditor as with any other debt.

Business Debt

If you own your business and the business is having financial difficulties, these difficulties may affect your personal financial situation as well.

Proprietorship or Partnership

As a new business, you may have entered into leases for space and other legal contracts. If operating as a sole proprietorship, you will be held personally responsible for any contract or agreement you enter into. Likewise, signing as a partner does not protect you from personal liability; all partners are usually responsible for partnership debt.

Corporation

You may have set up your business as a corporation, which is considered a separate, legal entity. Although a corporation usually shields its stockholders/owners from liability, you may still have *personal liability* as an officer or director.

Also, your creditors and landlords probably will require that you sign "personally," or that you *personally guarantee* the corporation's obligation. In other words, if the corporation goes out of business before it has met its obligation under a particular contract (for example, if the corporation vacates leased space before the end of the lease term), then you may be held personally liable for the remaining obligation.

As a defense against any action against you personally for your corporation's obligation, you will need to show that only the corporation signed the contract and that you signed as president (or other officer) of the corporation and not individually. (see Chapter 2.)

If you have signed a personal guarantee for any corporate obligation, determine whether it was for a secured debt. In other words, is the creditor able to take the collateral as payment for the balance owed? (Your guarantee may be *conditional*, requiring the creditor to first take the collateral, or *unconditional*, allowing the creditor to come directly to you for payment regardless of the collateral.)

While your guarantee of payment might not require the creditor to first take the collateral in satisfaction of the debt, the creditor may be willing to do so to minimize any potential losses, particularly if the creditor believes that you personally may not be able to pay the amount due.

Personal Guarantee

As for business leases that you have personally guaranteed, the landlord may be obligated to minimize its losses by finding another tenant as quickly as possible. (State laws vary on this issue.) However, any landlord attempting to obtain a judgment against you, personally, for the balance due on a lease may find the court much more receptive if he or she can show that he or she made a diligent effort to re-lease the space. You should do your best to help the landlord in finding a new tenant to minimize your liability under the guarantee. Even if the law does not require the landlord to attempt to minimize damages, your efforts may discourage the landlord from proceeding against you for the full amount due on the lease.

If there is any question as to whether the guarantee is legally valid and enforceable by the landlord, you should discuss this with an attorney.

Joint Liability

If you have signed a document for payment of an obligation containing the words *joint and several liability*, along with other owners of your business, do not assume that you will be responsible for repayment only to the extent of your share in the business. Joint and several liability means that each of those individuals who signed the document are individually, as well as jointly, liable for the total amount due. You may be liable for the entire amount due if the other *guarantors* do not pay.

Creditors usually pursue the signor with the greatest ability to repay the debt. If the creditor pursues you, make him aware of your personal financial situation. You may be able to reach an agreement with the creditor for payment, then pursue the other guarantors for *indemnification* or reimbursement.

Payroll Taxes

Aside from the corporate obligations you may have personally guaranteed, you must keep in mind that as an officer of the corporation, owner of the business, or partner in a partnership, you have other responsibilities and liabilities. The most important of these is payroll taxes.

As the business owner or authorized signer on the account from which payroll taxes are paid, you are personally obligated for the amount that the business deducted from the employees' wages and failed to send to the Internal Revenue Service (IRS). In other words, if your bookkeeper fails to make the deposits when due or if the business ceases operation and taxes are still owed, you may be held personally liable for payment.

Student Loans

The costs of college education are continually rising. More often than not, students must seek the help of student loans to finance their education. Various types of loans are available.

Federal Loan

If you had financial help with your college expenses through a student loan, chances are that repayment was guaranteed by the federal government. In other words, if the loan was made to you by a bank and you failed to pay, the bank looked to the federal government for the money.

Sallie Mae

Following either your graduation or withdrawal from school, you had a *grace period* (typically six months) before beginning to repay the loan. The bank, school, or other lender could collect the loan itself or could sell the loan to the *Student Loan Marketing Association* (SLMA, or "Sallie Mae") for collection. The SLMA is a corporation set up by the federal government for the purpose of collecting outstanding student loan obligations. The U.S. Department of Education may attempt to collect the balance due if SLMA is unsuccessful.

Both SLMA and the U.S. Department of Education will report your delinquent student loans to the credit reporting agencies (credit bureaus) and may take other action, such as to sue for collection or intercept your income tax refunds.

Default

If you are in *default* on a federally guaranteed loan, but are now able to start making payments, you may be able to bring the loan out of default by making a certain number of regular, consecutive monthly payments. Contact the guarantee agency that has your loan to find out how to bring the loan out of default.

Private Loan

If you borrowed money from your college or university and the loan was not federally guaranteed, the same options are open to the institution as to any other creditor, such as reporting your delinquent account to a credit reporting agency, hiring a collection agency, and filing a lawsuit. The school may also refuse to give your transcript and your diploma to you, as well as refuse to allow you to re-enroll. On the other hand, you have the same options as with any other creditor, including negotiating a smaller payment amount.

Your Options

Your options will depend upon the type of student loan. The types of federally guaranteed student loans include the following:
- *Perkins Loan* — based upon need, the loan is made by the school and with federal funds;
- *Stafford Loan – unsubsidized* (interest is charged from the date the loan is disbursed); and,
- *Stafford Loan – subsidized* (given on the basis of financial need; the interest is paid by the federal government until repayment begins). Find information at **http://studentaid.ed.gov** or **www.ed.gov**.

In addition, *Parent PLUS* loans assist parents in paying the expenses of an undergraduate student. U.S. Public Health Service loans are also available to students in health-related studies.

Each of these programs has its own unique rules regarding repayment and collection. Depending upon the type of loan you have, you may have one or more of the following options if you are unable to pay:

- cancellation of the loan;
- *deferment* of payments;
- negotiating for temporary suspension or reduction of payments;
- consolidating your loans; or,
- filing for bankruptcy (only in case of extreme hardship).

Cancellation

Again depending upon the type of loan, full or partial cancellation is generally available if you:

- die or become disabled;
- serve in the U.S. military;
- are employed full time as a nurse, medical technician, or law enforcement or corrections officer;
- are a Peace Corps or VISTA volunteer;
- are a Head Start program staff member;
- are a teacher in certain low-income areas; are a teacher of handicapped children; or, a teacher of math, science, foreign languages, or in other designated teacher-shortage areas; or,
- return to school to study at least half time.

For more information, call the holder of your loan or the Information Resource Center at the U.S. Department of Education at 800-872-5327.

Cancellation of the debt may also be possible in certain cases of fraud or misrepresentation by a trade school. In the past, there were numerous trade schools (for such occupations as truck driving, cosmetology, computer operation and repair, etc.) that got students to take out a government loan and turn the money over to the school, then closed the school before the course was completed. Other schools failed to provide sufficient education to allow the student to obtain employment once the course was completed.

If your trade school closed before you could complete the course of study, you were falsely certified to be eligible for the program, or you were entitled to a refund you never got, you may be able to have your loan cancelled. For more information, contact the Department of Education and ask for a list of closed schools, or contact your state's Attorney General's office.

Deferment

Typical situations in which *deferment* may be allowed are when you are:
- enrolled in school;
- unemployed;
- on active duty with the military or *National Oceanic and Atmoshpheric Administration*;
- a full-time teacher in a teacher-shortage area;
- disabled;
- completing an internship program;
- on parental leave;
- the mother of preschool children; or,
- suffering economic hardship.

Depending upon the type of loan, the deferment may be of both principle and interest, or of just principle (meaning you will have to make interest-only payments for the deferment period). For more information, contact your loan holder. Ask for a deferment application.

Negotiation

As with any other loan, you can always contact the holder of the loan, explain your situation, and try to arrange for payments to be temporarily suspended or reduced. If you do not have any luck negotiating an arrangement you can live with, contact your local consumer credit counseling service. They may be able to negotiate a better deal.

Consolidation

If you have more than one student loan, you may be able to consolidate them at a lower interest rate with a lower single payment, and possibly qualify for a deferment. Much will depend upon the types of loans you have and whether you are in default. For more information, contact the holder of your loan or Sallie Mae at 888-272-5543. The website for Sallie Mae is **www.salliemae.com**. You may also contact the U.S. Department of Education, Federal Direct Loan Program at 800-557-7392 or online at **www.ed.gov/about/offices/list/fsa/index.html**.

Bankruptcy

You will generally hear it said that student loans cannot be discharged in bankruptcy. A student loan may be discharged in bankruptcy only if repayment would cause extreme hardship. However, there are a couple of exceptions to this rule, and even if you cannot get a discharge, you may be able to get some indirect help.

It may be possible to have a student loan discharged in bankruptcy if the payments first became due more than seven years before filing for bankruptcy, or if you can convince the judge that repayment of the loan would cause you undue hardship. If you file for a repayment plan under Chapter 13 of the Bankruptcy Code and include your student loan in your repayment plan, it will at least stop lawsuits and other harassment over the delinquent loan.

If your school is withholding your transcript because of your nonpayment, it will have to release the transcript once you notify it of the bankruptcy proceeding, regardless of whether the debt is discharged.

Child Support

A child support obligation is not to be taken lightly. Congress has taken a special interest in payment of child support and addressed the problem of nonpayment by passing the *Federal Family Support Act of 1988* and the *Revised Uniform Reciprocal Enforcement of Support Act (URESA)*. In 1997, as part of the *Welfare Reform Act*, Congress passed the *Uniform Interstate*

Family Support Act (UIFSA), which is more streamlined and gives the states less latitude in enforcement as did the URESA. Under UIFSA, the district attorney in your state will be contacted by the district attorney in your spouse's state regarding the child support due. The district attorney in your state will then pursue you for the amount.

The law requires your employer to honor a court order to withhold the support payment from your wages. (You can also agree with the other parent or guardian of the child to pay directly.) You can also be ordered to go to jail for contempt of court if you fail to pay child support.

NOTE: *In some states, you may be charged with a misdemeanor.*

Modification

If you simply cannot pay the amount ordered by the court, then you should file a request for modification, explaining the circumstances and why you believe the amount should be reduced. In all states, you will generally need to show that your income has decreased so that you are no longer able to pay the amount originally ordered.

A sample *Motion for Modification* is found at the end of Chapter 15, with examples of reasons for the request. This sample form shows you how simple it can be to ask for a decrease in child support. You should also obtain a copy of your state's support guidelines.

Depending upon your state, the guidelines will be in either the statutes, court rules, or a document from some state agency. If you cannot find them in the statutes or court rules, request a copy from the court clerk or child support enforcement agency. You may find that you are paying more than the guidelines require. If so, you can request a modification.

Judgment

If your spouse gets a judgment against you for past-due child support, that judgment may also be collected like any other judgment and the same time periods for collection may apply. (see Chapter 16.)

Income Tax Refund

In addition, your income tax refunds may be intercepted and applied to your past due child support. If this occurs, you will receive a notice of the impending tax intercept. The notice will advise you of your right to request some kind of hearing to challenge the taking of your tax refund, and how to go about getting a hearing.

Generally, you will only be able to stop the intercept if you have already paid what is owed, or are making regular payments pursuant to an agreement you made for payment of the past due amount (of course, other unusual circumstances may also avoid an intercept, but these are so varied and unusual that they cannot be covered here).

If you are remarried and some of the tax refund is for the income of your current spouse, you can apply to the IRS for your spouse's share of the refund. Contact the IRS to obtain the proper form at either 800-829-1040 or at their website at **www.irs.gov**.

Chapter 3

Your Credit Report

The *Fair Credit Reporting Act* (FCRA) as amended September 30, 1997, regulates the activities of credit reporting agencies. (U.S.C., Title 15, Sec. 1601.) A credit reporting agency, also known as a credit bureau and called *consumer reporting agency* under this law, means any person or business that assembles or evaluates consumer credit information for the purpose of providing consumer reports (commonly known as *credit reports*) to third parties. Under the Fair Credit Reporting Act, *consumer* means an individual. You, as the person whose credit is being reported, are the consumer.

Information a Consumer Reporting Agency May Furnish

A reporting agency may furnish your credit report only under the following circumstances provided for by law:

- in response to a court order;
- in accordance with written instructions from the consumer;
- to any person that the reporting agency has reason to believe:
  - is involved in the extension of credit to, or review or collection of an account of the consumer;
  - intends to use the information for employment purposes;
  - intends to use the information in connection with the underwriting of insurance involving the consumer;

- intends to use the information in connection with a determination of the consumer's eligibility for a license or other benefit granted by a governmental agency (if the agency is required by law to consider an applicant's financial responsibility or status);
- otherwise has a legitimate business need for the information in connection with a business transaction involving the consumer; or,
- in certain cases involving child support issues.

Obtaining Information from the Agency's Files

The contents of your credit report can affect your ability to get a loan as well as employment. As a consumer, upon request and proper identification, you have the right to obtain the following information in the reporting agency's files:

- the nature and substance of all information (except medical information) in the agency's file on the consumer at the time of the request;
- the sources of the information (except as to information acquired solely for use in preparing an investigative consumer report and used for no other purpose, which is beyond the scope of this book);
- the recipients of any consumer report on the consumer that the reporting agency has furnished:
  - for employment purposes within the two-year period preceding the request, and
  - for any other purpose within the six-month period preceding the request.

The agency is required to provide you the requested information during normal business hours and on reasonable notice. The information should be provided to you in person if you have proper identification, or by telephone if you have made written request and have proper identification. If long distance, you must pay for the call.

The agency must have trained personnel explain to you any questions you have about the report. If you make the request in person and have someone with you, the agency must have written permission from you to disclose any information in your companion's presence. The three major national credit bureaus are:

Equifax
P.O. Box 740241
Atlanta, GA 30374
800-685-1111
www.equifax.com

Experian
475 Anton Boulevard
Costa Mesa, CA 92626
888-397-3742
www.experian.com

TransUnion
P.O. Box 2000
Chester, PA 19022
800-888-4213
www.transunion.com

Items Your Credit Report Cannot Contain
By law, your credit report cannot contain any of the following:
- a discharge or final order in bankruptcy court dated more than ten years prior to the date of the credit report;
- lawsuits and judgments entered more than seven years prior to the date of the credit report. (However, if the applicable statute of limitations is longer than seven years, lawsuits and judgments may stay on the credit report until the applicable statute of limitations expire. For example, if your state allows a judgment to remain in effect for a period of ten years, then the ten-year period may apply, instead of the seven-year period.);
- paid tax liens that, from the date of payment, precede the report by more than seven years;

- accounts placed for collection or charged to profit and loss by the creditor that are dated more than seven years before the credit report;
- records of arrest, indictment, or conviction of crime that, from date of disposition, release, or parole, precede the report by more than seven years; and,
- any other adverse information that precedes the report by more than seven years except that default information concerning U.S. Government insured or guaranteed student loans can be reported for seven years, after actions to collect the debt have been taken against certain guarantors.

However, these restrictions do not apply if the report is to be used in connection with:
- a credit transaction involving, or that may reasonably be expected to involve, a principal amount of $150,000 or more;
- the underwriting of life insurance involving, or that may reasonably be expected to involve, a face amount of $150,000 or more; or,
- the employment of any individual at an annual salary that equals, or that may reasonably be expected to equal, $75,000 or more.

The "Quick Fix"

You may be told by a so-called credit repair company that you will not be able to get credit for ten years after you have filed for bankruptcy. Such companies are regulated under the *Credit Repair Organizations Act*. (U.S.C., Title 15, Chapter 41.) If you have been granted bankruptcy, you might receive correspondence from credit repair companies explaining that you will be unable to get loans, credit cards, etc. This, of course, is not necessarily correct. It may be suggested that the credit repair company can help you hide your bankruptcy by essentially providing you with a new credit history.

> **Warning:** To help you *hide* your bankruptcy, the credit repair company may promise to tell you how, for a fee, to establish a new credit identity. The plan, however, is illegal. If you use the plan, often called *file segregation*, you could face fines or even prison.

If the company offers to assist you in hiding your bankruptcy and establish a new credit identity, beware that this is probably illegal, particularly if you apply for a new tax identification number to use in place of your Social Security number, using a new address and credit references.

Remember that no one can legally remove correct negative information from your credit report. However, the law does allow you the opportunity to ask that incorrect or incomplete information be reviewed as explained in this chapter. You can also submit a letter of explanation that can be included with a copy of your credit report. There is no charge for this. Anything that a so-called credit repair service can do for you legally, you can do for yourself at little or no cost.

Disputing Items in Your Report

The information contained in credit reports is obtained from a variety of sources, including local court records and businesses who pay a fee to the credit bureau. If you dispute the accuracy of any of the information in your credit report, do the following.

- Let the reporting agency know of your dispute of the specific information. At that time, the agency must, within a reasonable period of time, reinvestigate and record the current status of that information. If it has reasonable grounds to believe that your dispute is frivolous or irrelevant, then they may be exempted.
- If after the reinvestigation the information is found to be inaccurate or can no longer be verified by the agency, then the agency must promptly delete the information from your report. Contradictory information in the file cannot be used by the agency as reasonable grounds for believing your dispute is frivolous or irrelevant. (See the sample letter on page 30.) According to the law, if you disagree with

an entry on your credit report and the creditor placing the information on the report cannot verify that it is correct, then the credit reporting service must remove that information.

- If the reinvestigation does not resolve the dispute, you may file a brief statement setting forth the nature of the dispute. The agency may limit the statement to not more than one hundred words if agency personnel provide you with assistance in writing a clear summary of the dispute.

- Whenever you file a statement of dispute, unless there are reasonable grounds for the agency to believe your statement is frivolous or irrelevant, the agency must clearly note in any subsequent report containing the information that it is disputed. It must provide either your statement or a clear and accurate summary of your statement. (See the sample letter on page 31.)

> **Example:** John and Sandy made a loan application to purchase a new home. The credit report reflected nonpayment of a doctor bill approximately a year previously. John and Sandy thought their insurance company had paid the outstanding bill, and immediately made arrangements to pay once they realized this reflected negatively on their credit report. They also sent a letter to the reporting agency clarifying the reason for nonpayment and stating that acceptable arrangements had been made with the physician to pay the bill. They were then given the mortgage they had applied for.

- Following the agency's removal of any information that is found to be inaccurate, whose accuracy can no longer be verified, or any notation in the agency's file as to disputed information, the agency must, at your request, (1) either furnish notification that the item has been deleted or (2) send the statement or summary regarding a disputed item to any person who is specifically designated by you and who has within the past two years received your credit report for employment purposes, or within the last six months received your credit report for any other purposes.

The agency must clearly and conspicuously disclose to you your rights to make such a request. The agency's disclosure must be made at or before the time the information is removed or your statement regarding the disputed information is received.

Cost of the Report

You may now request a free copy of your credit report through the Federal Trade Commission at **www.ftc.gov/bcp/online/edcams/credit/coninfo_reports.htm**. It must also be provided free of charge from the reporting agency your report came from if:

- you request it within sixty days of notice that your credit has been or may be adversely affected;
- you request it within sixty days of notice that you have been denied employment; or,
- if credit or insurance rates are increased due to the report.

Credit reporting services are limited in the amount they can charge for a copy of your credit report. Most will provide a variety of different information so prices will vary depending on what exactly you request to receive. Each of the big three reporting agencies must provide you one free copy per year of your credit report. You can contact them directly or go to **www.annualcreditreport.com** to obtain your free copy. This copy is limited in the information it provides, so you may wish to supplement it with one that may cost you a few (well-spent) dollars. It is a good idea for you to obtain a copy once a year to be sure of accuracy.

If you receive welfare, are out of work and looking for a job, or have been the victim of credit card fraud (someone has stolen and used your card), you must be provided a copy of your credit report upon request at no charge. The agency also cannot charge for the deletion of any information that is determined to be inaccurate.

Reports for Employment Purposes

Under the law, a prospective employer must have your written permission before getting a copy of your credit report. A reporting agency that furnishes a report for employment purposes that contains items of information that are matters of public record and are likely to have an adverse effect upon your ability to obtain employment must:

- at the time such information is reported to a prospective employer, notify you of the fact that public record information is being reported by the consumer reporting agency, together with the name and address of the person to whom such information is being reported, and

- maintain strict procedures designed to insure that whenever public record information that is likely to have an adverse effect on your ability to obtain employment is reported, it is complete and up to date. Items relating to arrests, indictments, convictions, suits, tax liens, and outstanding judgments are considered up to date if the current public record status of the item at the time of the report is reported.

Reports Containing Medical Information

The law restricts a credit reporting agency from furnishing a credit report that contains any medical information for employment, credit, insurance, or direct marketing transaction purposes without first obtaining your consent.

Requirements for Users of Reports

Whenever credit or insurance for personal, family, household purposes, or employment is denied, or the charge for such credit or insurance is increased because of information contained in a report from a reporting agency, the user of the report must advise you of that situation. It must also supply the name and address of the consumer reporting agency making the report.

Businesses sometimes create mailing lists of prospective new customers based on information contained in credit reports, and make firm offers of credit or insurance based on this information. (For example, you may receive offers of a specified line of credit from credit card companies through the mail.)

The law requires that a single toll-free number be established by the three major credit reporting services—Equifax, TransUnion, and Experian—so that consumers may prohibit the use of their credit reports for credit or insurance transactions that are not initiated by the customer. A notice of election form should be provided to you for completion and signature. The election will be effective only for a two-year period if you do not submit the notice of election form. (Each of the three major credit reporting services also has its own toll-free number.)

Use of Other Information

Sometimes credit for personal, family, or household purposes is denied, or the charge for such credit is increased either wholly or in part because of information obtained from a person other than a consumer reporting agency. This affects your creditworthiness, credit standing, credit capacity, character, general reputation, personal characteristics, or mode of living, and the user of such information must, within a reasonable period of time after receiving your written request, disclose the nature of the information to you. The user must receive your written request within sixty days of your learning of the adverse action. At the time the user of the information tells you about the adverse action, he must also clearly and accurately disclose your rights to make the written request.

Obtaining Information under False Pretenses

Anyone who knowingly and willfully obtains information about a consumer from a reporting agency under false pretenses can be fined not more than $5,000 or imprisoned not more than two years, or both.

Providing Information to an Unauthorized Person

Any officer or employee of a reporting agency who knowingly and willfully provides information concerning an individual from the agency's files to a person not authorized to receive that information can be fined up to $5,000, imprisoned up to one year, or both.

Reporting Agency Liability for Noncompliance

A credit reporting agency may either: comply with the law, which is generally the case, and make an unintentional error (negligent noncompliance), or intentionally violate the law (willful noncompliance). Willful noncompliance carries the greatest penalty.

Negligent Noncompliance

A reporting agency or user of information provided by a reporting agency that negligently fails to comply with any requirement under the Consumer Credit Act is liable to you in an amount equal to the sum of:

- any actual damages suffered by you as a result of the failure and
- in the case of any successful action to enforce any liability under the applicable section of the Consumer Credit Act, the costs of the action together with reasonable attorney's fees as determined by the court.

Willful Noncompliance

A reporting agency or user of information provided by a reporting agency that willfully fails to comply with the legal requirements is liable to you under the FCRA in an amount equal to the sum of:

- any actual damages suffered by you as a result of the failure;
- such amount of punitive damages as the court may allow; and,
- in the case of any successful action to enforce any liability under this section, the costs of the action together with reasonable attorney's fees as determined by the court.

Your Remedies

If you believe a credit reporting agency has failed to comply with any of the requirements under the Consumer Credit Act, particularly the FCRA, you may have recourse. For example, consumers have been awarded damages for embarrassment and humiliation as a result of a reporting agency negligently furnishing an inaccurate mortgage report. A consumer has also been awarded damages for mental anguish when he had to leave his employment numerous times to meet with the agency as a result of its refusal to disclose information to him about his credit report.

Time Limitations

You may bring an action against the agency within two years from the date the liability arises; except, where the agency has willfully misrepresented any information required to be disclosed and the information misrepresented is necessary to establish the agency's liability, the action may be brought within two years after discovery of the misrepresentation.

The Federal Trade Commission (FTC) is the federal agency given the authority to enforce the provisions of the Fair Credit Reporting Act. You may register a complaint at the office in your district. (see Appendix B.) You should send your complaint in writing, with a copy of the letter going to the credit reporting agency. (See the sample letter on page 32.) The complaint should be sent to:

Consumer Response Center, FCRA
Federal Trade Commission
Washington, DC 20580

For Further Research

The Federal Trade Commission has detailed information about credit reporting agencies, and the rules that govern them, available at its website at **www.ftc.gov**.

You should also contact your state's consumer affairs office for additional information.

Sample Letter Requesting
Removal of Information

August 12, 2007

Credit Bureau
321 Broad Street
Your Town, USA

                                    RE: Credit Report for Jane Doe
                                    Social Security No. 555-55-5555

Dear Sir or Madam:

On August 3, 2007, I was notified that credit had been denied me because of an entry on my credit report.

The credit report showed that I failed to make payment in the amount of $50.00 to a Dr. Payne. You must have me confused with another Jane Doe, as I do not know a Dr. Payne, nor have I ever used his services.

Please delete this entry from my credit report. Thank you.

Sincerely,
Jane Doe
CERTIFIED MAIL
RETURN RECEIPT REQUESTED
P-298-335-482

Sample Letter Reporting
Inaccurate Credit Information

August 12, 2007

Credit Bureau
321 Broad Street
Your Town, USA

                              RE: Credit Report for Jane Doe
                              Social Security No. 555-55-5555

Dear Sir or Madam:

In applying for a mortgage, it was brought to my attention that there is an entry on my credit report showing that I owe Dr. Feilgoodt a balance of $300.

The $300 was for medical treatment approximately one year ago. It was my understanding that this amount had been paid by my insurance company along with other medical bills incurred at that time. I did not receive a bill for this amount after giving the medical center business office information about my insurance policy.

I intend to pay Dr. Feilgoodt's bill in full as soon as possible. Please include this letter in my credit report file. Thank you.

Sincerely,
Jane Doe
CERTIFIED MAIL
RETURN RECEIPT REQUESTED
P-298-335-482

Sample Letter Complaining to FTC

August 12, 2007

Federal Trade Commission
1718 Peachtree Street, NW
Room 1000
Atlanta, GA 30367

RE: Credit Bureau
321 Broad Street
Your Town, USA

Dear Sir or Madam:

On June 1, 2007, I notified Credit Bureau, in writing, that an entry on my credit report was incorrect, and asked that it be deleted.

The credit report showed that I failed to make payment in the amount of $50.00 to a Dr. Payne. Apparently Credit Bureau has me confused with another Jane Doe, as I do not know a Dr. Payne, nor have I ever used his services.

Credit Bureau refused to follow up on my letter, and the entry still shows on my credit report without an explanation or notice that it is disputed.

I wish to file a complaint against Credit Bureau under the Fair Credit Reporting Act.

Sincerely,
Jane Doe
cc: Credit Bureau

Chapter 4

Establishing Good Credit

We are all tempted to spend money, and if we don't have the money readily available, we are tempted to buy *on credit*, or borrow. Chapter 1 explained that extending and using credit is vital to our lives and our economy. Even if we buy only necessities on credit and pay our outstanding balance in full every month, it is important that we have credit available to us. This requires that we first establish a good credit history.

In case of a bankruptcy or other major financial setback that results in a bad or negative credit history, it is important that we reestablish good credit. The following sections describe the contents of a credit history and how to begin establishing or reestablishing good credit.

Credit History

Your credit history is contained primarily in your credit report. It is a compilation of information gathered primarily from your lenders. (Credit reports and credit bureaus were described and explained in more detail in Chapter 3.) Without a good *credit history* (an individual's record of loans and repayment patterns including bankruptcies and judgments), it is often difficult to obtain a loan. For example, a teenager who buys his first car will probably need to borrow some of the money. Since he or she has no credit history, a bank may decide the loan would be too great a risk and deny the application. This is often the case in spite of the fact that an applicant has a good job with income more than adequate to make the payments. Therefore, it is extremely important that individuals begin early to establish a good credit record.

Savings and Checking Accounts

The first step in establishing good credit is opening a savings and checking account. A *debit card* is simply another method of deducting money from your checking account for purchases and thus not really credit (nor is its use reported to the credit bureau). However, it is one way to begin managing your money responsibly. The next step is obtaining some type of loan, repayment of which is reported to the credit bureau under your name and Social Security number.

Credit Cards

Young adults, particularly college students without a credit history, often receive offers from banks and other businesses for credit cards. The terms offered should be studied carefully. These will typically extend a lower amount of credit, perhaps $300 or $500. Accepting one of these credit cards, using it sparingly, and making sure the payments are made before the due date, is a good way to begin establishing a credit history. After proving that you are responsible with credit, your good credit history will allow you to choose other credit cards, perhaps with lower interest rates and higher credit limits.

Secured Credit Cards

Others may be able to begin their personal credit record by obtaining a *secured credit card* from their bank. The money in a savings or deposit account will be used as security for payment of the amounts charged on the credit card account.

Secured credit cards are also offered by lenders nationally who require a deposit, typically between $300 and $500, per application. Information about secured credit cards can be found on the Internet, including the website **www.bankrate.com**.

After a year or more of making payments on the secured credit card on time, the lender may be willing to give an unsecured card with a higher dollar limit. Some banks may refuse to issue even a secured credit card to individuals who have recently filed for bankruptcy or have federal tax liens. As with any other consumer product, fees vary and it is important to comparison shop. The federal *Truth in Lending Act* requires disclosure of financing terms and costs by all companies offering consumer credit. You should know how much your credit will cost before you obligate yourself.

Retail Store Credit Cards

Another way to begin a good credit history is by using a local retail store credit card. Make sure your lender reports your use of the card and payment record to a credit bureau. Other lenders will request your payment history from the credit bureau before granting additional credit.

In some cases, people who have completed bankruptcy proceedings and whose debts have been discharged by the bankruptcy court may receive unsolicited offers for new credit cards. The credit card companies apparently recognize that the individual is virtually debt-free following the bankruptcy court discharge, and therefore will have more income with which to make future credit card payments. Keeping in mind that one must wait at least seven years before filing for bankruptcy again, it is extremely important to follow the rules for responsible use of credit.

Bank Loans

Your local bank may be willing to extend credit to you, either because the bank knows you or your family personally, or because you have some *collateral* that can be temporarily signed over to the bank until the loan is repaid. You should make an appointment with the banker. Be prepared with your application worksheet and explain how and when you expect to repay. Be sure the lender will be reporting your loan and prompt payment to the credit bureaus to make sure it becomes part of your credit history.

Cosigned Loans

Another possibility for establishing good credit is with the help of a *cosigner*. For example, in the case of a teenager buying his or her first car, the father may *cosign* the loan, guaranteeing payment in the event his son or daughter does not meet the obligations. If he or she pays as required by the terms of the loan, he or she will have started the process of establishing a good credit history. Although it might be more difficult to find someone who is willing to cosign if you are trying to reestablish credit following a bankruptcy, you may consider providing the cosigner with security in another asset as assurance that you will pay the loan.

Education Loans

Loans are also available for higher education purposes. The applications and requirements will vary with the type of loan. One of the best places to begin this loan process is at the financial aid office of the school or college. Repayment usually doesn't begin until completing or leaving the school program. This is another good opportunity to establish your credit history.

Making Payments

Once you have received a new credit card or obtained a loan, the importance of making payments on time cannot be emphasized enough. Remember that the lender or credit card company must receive payment on or before the due date. The date you mail the payment doesn't matter, as long as it is received by the due date shown on your statement or loan document. If the payment is lost in the mail, it is your responsibility — not the lender's. Although it takes time and a few extra dollars, some people send their payments by certified mail, return receipt requested.

Other lenders offer a *telepay system*, by which the lender — prompted by you (often an automated system) — deducts a specified amount from your bank account. Another payment method might be by *automatic withdrawal* from your bank account. (Some mortgages are set up in this manner.) If you set up an automatic withdrawal system, you must make sure that your account always has sufficient funds on deposit to cover the payment amount. Failure to meet your obligations will result in a negative notation on your credit report. This information will be used to determine whether you are a good credit risk in the future, as well as a good employee, tenant, association member, etc.

A credit history with a less than perfect payment record may also result in higher costs if a lender does in fact provide credit. For example, the recent low mortgage interest rates have encouraged many to *refinance* their homes. However, someone with a bad credit history would most likely be required to pay a higher rate, and therefore not be able to take advantage of the potential savings.

Credit Application Process

Mortgage loans, equity lines of credit, automobile loans, and particularly credit cards are advertised constantly. (Credit card offers are often made by mail.) It is important to understand the differences. Fees, rates, calculation of interest, benefits such as airline miles, purchase protection insurance, rewards, etc. will vary from one type of card to another. Understand the terms before using the credit. Be particularly cautious about low initial rates, which may increase significantly at a later date.

All credit, whether in the form of a credit card or loan from a bank, is given with specific terms and conditions that are detailed in the loan documents. Credit card terms are contained in the application form that must be signed and returned to the issuing company. The form contains details regarding payment due dates, grace periods, interest rates, etc.

A bank loan typically requires that you sign a promissory note that contains the terms of repayment, leases require disclosures by the lessor, and a mortgage requires numerous disclosures by the lender. These are discussed in detail in Chapters 11 and 12. Before committing yourself to any loan obligations, be sure you completely understand the terms.

An application for credit typically requires that you provide the lender certain information:

- your name;
- Social Security number;

- name and address of employer;
- number of years employed by current employer (and previous employment information if not in your current position for several years);
- home address;
- whether you rent or own;
- a list and value of other assets; and,
- a list of liabilities.

When making the application, you will be authorizing the lender to obtain and review a copy of your credit report that contains your credit history, as well as any judgments, tax, or other liens, and bankruptcies. The credit report will also show how much you currently owe; how much you charge on a monthly basis; and, your *credit limit* on each account (the amount of credit available to you). You may also be requested to list bank and other references such as your landlord, whom the lender may call to verify your loan and payment history.

Credit Scoring

A system called *credit scoring* is used by some lenders to assist in determining whether you qualify for credit and, if so, under what terms. A *credit profile* is then assembled. This profile includes information about:

- the number and types of your credit accounts;
- the total of your outstanding balances;
- the amount of credit available to you;
- whether you pay your bills on time;
- whether any of your accounts have been sent for collection (see Chapter 7); and,
- how long you have had your accounts.

Each item is assigned a certain number of points. The total points are supposed to indicate how likely you are to repay and whether you will make your payments on time. Your employment history, whether you rent or own your home, and other factors may also be used in determining your credit score.

The *Equal Credit Opportunity Act* (ECOA) does not allow use of sex, race, marital status, religion, or national origin as factors. (If you believe you have been denied credit in violation of the ECOA, you should contact either the Federal Trade Commission or a private attorney.)

If a lender denies your application for credit, the lender must either give you notice explaining the specific reasons or give you the opportunity to inquire about the reasons within sixty days from the date of denial. Once you know why your application was denied, you can begin taking the necessary steps to improve your credit history. For example, you may need to close some accounts that you do not use but that affect your score, or you may need to pay off some balances.

When attempting to reestablish credit, you should first request a copy of your credit report to avoid any surprises. You may request a copy from any of the three credit reporting companies:

- **Equifax** — 800-685-1111
- **Experian** — 888-397-3742
- **TransUnion** — 800-888-4213

Since your lender will order and review your credit report in determining whether to approve your credit application, you should be prepared to explain any negative entries. (Credit reporting errors are discussed in Chapter 3.)

Credit Approval

If your application for a credit card or other type of loan is approved, the total amount you can charge or borrow will be limited. The amount of the credit limit will depend upon a number of factors, including your income, the information contained on your credit report, your employment history, the value of your assets, and the information gathered by the lender from other sources, such as your landlord.

If you are applying for credit for the first time or reapplying following a bankruptcy, the annual fees (if any) and interest rates may be higher than you would otherwise pay because the lender considers you a higher credit risk. Once you've proven that you can, in fact, handle credit responsibly, shop around for credit with lower costs.

An important resource which contains a wealth of information for obtaining and managing good credit is the Federal Trade Commission website, at **www.ftc.gov/bcp/conline/edcams/credit/coninfo_loans.htm**.

Chapter 5

Using Credit Responsibly

Once you've received a credit card or been granted a loan, you should keep the documents detailing payment terms in a safe place in case you need to refer to them at a later date. Make a note to yourself of the payment due dates.

Following are some guidelines for using credit responsibly.

- Know the terms of your loan, whether credit card, equity line of credit (a loan using equity in property as security), car loan, lease, simple consumer loan, or mortgage.
- Keep a copy of all credit cards and a list of the telephone numbers for each lender.
- Carry only one or two credit cards in your purse or wallet.
- Make *at least* the required minimum payment every month.
- Send in your payment in plenty of time for it to reach the lender on or before the due date. (If you're concerned about the payment reaching the creditor on time, consider sending it by a courier service or electronic funds transfer. This will likely be less costly than a late payment fee.)
- Keep a copy or record of your payment.
- Keep track of your spending habits, making every effort that the amount you spend on credit card debt and consumer loans does not exceed 20% of your income.
- Do not make unnecessary purchases using a credit card. (By the time the payment is due, you might not want or need the item.)

- If you cannot pay your credit card balance in full every month, use the card only for emergencies or major purchases.
- Never charge to the limit on credit cards unless you are able to pay the full or a large portion of the outstanding balance when you receive the statement.
- Review your credit card or loan statement every month to make sure it accurately reflects your payments and charges.
- If your statements contain errors, contact the credit card company or lender immediately. Follow up with a letter sent certified mail with receipt requested. Time limitations for contesting charges are explained in your loan documents and on your credit card statements. (If you miss the deadline, you may find yourself responsible for the incorrect charge.)
- Keep track of your credit cards. If one is lost or stolen, report it immediately to the telephone number you have written on your list and follow-up with a letter.
- *Most important — stay in control of your finances and credit. Do not allow your spending habits to control you.*

If an emergency requiring the extensive use of credit does arise, try working out payment arrangements directly with the service provider — for example, the physician instead of a credit card company to whom you might charge the physician's fees.

Of course, there are situations that might cause someone to use too much credit. For various reasons, some people find themselves unable to control their spending and meet their financial obligations. Section II of this book more fully explains the various types of credit, as well as the federal and state laws enacted to fully inform and protect consumers from unscrupulous lenders. It also provides the necessary tools for those who have disputes with their lenders or who have debt that they no longer pay.

NOTE: *Freddie Mac, the government-backed mortgage company, has an educational course titled A Curriculum to Help Consumers Understand, Build, and Maintain Better Credit on its website. You can access it at **www.freddiemac.com/ creditsmart/home.html**.*

Section II

UNDERSTANDING

CREDIT PITFALLS

Chapter 6

Strategies Before Creditors and Collectors Call

As soon as you realize that you may have difficulties in making your payments, you should contact your creditors. Do not try to hide your financial condition. Let them know what has happened—job layoff, divorce, illness, etc.—and that you will make every effort to meet your financial obligations. Offer to make minimal payments for a period of time, or perhaps *suspend* your payments (not make any) for a month or more.

Prepare Yourself and Your Creditors

Generally, your creditors will be much more receptive to your suggestions for reduced or suspended payments if you notify them before they find it necessary to contact you. (Many will accept token payments instead of pursuing collection, as long as you explain the reasons for your inability to pay, and that you will make up the difference as soon as you are able.)

Prioritize

You should also take stock of your current financial situation and place your debts and assets in order of priority. (see Chapter 13.) Your most important obligations may be your mortgage or rent, utilities, and car payment. Consider what you can sell in order to pay off some of your debt. Practical strategies, although perhaps a bit difficult to accept at first, will help see you through the tough times.

Perhaps you should sell your car, pay off the loan, and buy an older, used car, which would also lower your insurance premium. However, before selling any property to pay your debt, be sure you understand what will be exempt from judgment creditors and bankruptcy in your state. (see Chapter 17.)

The "Minimum One Dollar Payment" Myth

Some people have the mistaken notion that a payment of one dollar per month is sufficient—particularly when it comes to hospital and doctor bills—and that no action can be taken by the creditor if that one dollar payment is made regularly. This is an incorrect assumption. Those creditors have the right to receive payment from you in the manner you agreed to pay them, or in a timely manner.

If you cannot reach an agreement with your creditor as to how a past-due account can be paid, or if you reach an agreement and then do not pay, the creditor can send the past-due account to a collection agency, and ultimately (or in some cases directly) to the credit bureau. The creditor may also choose to pursue a judgment against you, often in a small claims court where cases can be handled without a lawyer. However, if your creditor refuses to work with you during your period of financial difficulties, then you may have a more sympathetic judge when you appear in court.

Wage Assignments

Be wary if a creditor asks you to assign some of your wages to make the payments on the loan. This may be illegal in certain cases under federal law, and it effectively reduces your control over your income. Wage assignments in non-real estate transactions are allowed only if you are also given the power to revoke the assignment. (Code of Federal Regulations (C.F.R.), Title 16, Section (Sec.) 444.2.)

Credit Counseling

If you find yourself in credit trouble, *credit counseling* can often be helpful. Consumer credit counseling is available through local offices affiliated with the National Foundation for Consumer Credit. This is a national network of over 1,450 Neighborhood Financial Care Centers. It is a nonprofit organization, supported by contributions from banks, consumer finance companies, merchants, credit unions, etc. A consumer credit counseling service can work with your creditors to establish a realistic payment program. You may find information about the services or locate your nearest center on the Internet at **www.nfcc.org**.

HUD Counseling

There are approximately 750 HUD (Housing and Urban Development) approved counseling agencies all over the country. If you are unable to make payments under a Federal Housing Administration (FHA) mortgage, you will be referred to such an agency. However, counseling assistance is available to anyone, usually at no charge. The counselors can help you get employment, budget your income, and work out your credit difficulties. You may call 800-569-4287 for a referral to your local HUD-approved counseling agency or call 800-767-7468 for additional information. You can also find information at **www.hudhcc.org**.

Chapter 7

When the Collection Agency Calls

A *collection agency* is a business that collects outstanding bills for other businesses.

If, after sending past-due notices and perhaps telephoning, a creditor is unable to collect an outstanding bill from you, the creditor may contract with a collection agency to collect the bill. If this happens, the creditor will give the agency a commission from the amount collected (usually 50%), with the remaining amount then paid to the creditor. The creditor may also sell your account to the collection agency at a discount. When the account has been sold to the agency, the agency can sue on its own behalf to collect the amount due.

NOTE: *Child support payments are not "debts" covered by the Fair Debt Collection Practices Act, which is discussed in this chapter.*

What a Collection Agency Can Do

Beyond sending letters and calling, there is little a collection agency can do to collect a debt. An agency collector once said, "...if people knew their legal rights, collection agencies might find it difficult to stay in business." You should be aware that if a collection agency is a member of a credit reporting service, then your unpaid debt may be reported and may be reflected on your credit report for a period of seven years. Since the collection agency gets paid only on the amounts collected, the collector may use various (and possibly illegal) tactics to get payment from you.

Collection agency practices are regulated by the *Fair Debt Collection Practices Act* (FDCPA).

The Fair Debt Collection Practices Act is a federal law also known as Public Law 95-109. Congress passed this law to regulate collection agencies and help eliminate abusive debt collection practices that contributed to loss of jobs and invasion of privacy.

If a collection agency violates any of the provisions of the law in attempting to collect a debt from you, you may have civil remedies available to you, including *punitive damages.* (In order for the Act to apply, the debt must have been incurred for personal, family, or household purposes.)

The Federal Trade Commission is the federal agency responsible for regulating collection agencies. Under the FDCPA, an attorney or law firm can be considered a collection agency if it regularly engages in the collection of debts allegedly owed by consumers.

The First Call from a Collector

Before or no later than five days after your first call from the collection agency, the collector must send you a written notice containing:
- the amount of the debt you supposedly owe;
- the name of the creditor to whom the debt is owed;
- a statement that, unless you dispute the validity of the debt within thirty days, the debt will be assumed to be valid;
- a statement that, if you notify the collector in writing within the thirty-day period that the debt, or any portion of it, is disputed, the collector will get verification and mail it to you; and,
- a statement that, upon your written request within the thirty-day period, the collector will provide you with the name of the original creditor if different from the current creditor.

Any communication you receive from the collector must clearly state that the purpose of the communication is to collect a debt, and that any information obtained will be used for that purpose.

You have thirty days after receipt of the notice from the collection agency to respond. Send a letter back to the agency stating that you do not agree with all or part of the bill, and why, in your opinion, you do not owe the money. (See page 61 for a sample letter.)

NOTE: *Any subsequent communication by the collector regarding the debt must also include the fact that you have disputed the debt.*

The collection agency must then stop all attempts to collect the debt from you until the debt is verified by the creditor and a copy of the verification is sent to you. You may demand that the collector notify any person who received notice of the debt from him within the previous ninety-day period that the debt has been disputed.

If you do not dispute the debt in writing within the thirty-day period, the collection agency can assume you agree that the amount stated in the notice is accurate, and can continue its collection efforts.

When you receive a call or letter from a collection agency attempting to collect a debt you owed to someone else, there are a number of things you can do. Most importantly, you can simply write a letter and ask that you not be contacted anymore. (See page 60 for a sample of this type of letter.) This, by law, should be enough. However, some collectors use very aggressive and sometimes abusive tactics in order to get payments.

What a Collection Agency Cannot Do

The following is a list of collection agency practices that are among those prohibited under the Fair Debt Collection Practices Act (FDCPA), with suggestions as to what you can do if you believe an agency has violated a provision of the Act.

Remember that these apply to collection agencies and not the creditor to whom the debt may be owed. While the creditor cannot harass you, he or she is not subject to the same regulations as collection agencies. (Several states regulate the activities of creditors as well.)

These are items that the FDCPA states the collection agencies cannot do. The statements are summarized.

FDCPA STATEMENT: *A collection agency representative should not lead you to believe in any manner that he is a law enforcement officer or a representative of any governmental agency. A debt collector is prohibited from using a police badge or other symbol of authority.*

RESPONSE: If you are contacted by a debt collector using these tactics, make sure you get his name and place of employment to use in any action against him.

FDCPA STATEMENT: *A collection agency representative must not use or threaten force, violence, or other criminal means to harm you, your reputation, or property.*

RESPONSE: If a debt collector threatens to cause you harm, then you should, if possible, record the conversation and advise the collector that you are doing so, or ask a friend to listen to the call on an extension phone. Some collection agencies record telephone conversations their collectors have with debtors in order to minimize these violations.

FDCPA STATEMENT: *A collection agency representative must not communicate with other people (except your lawyer or a consumer reporting agency) about your account without your prior consent, except to the extent reasonably necessary to enforce a court order.*

RESPONSE: If a collector violates this law, have the individual to whom the information was disclosed write down that information, sign it, and have it notarized. You may then use this to support your complaint to the appropriate governmental office. You may also have a claim for damages.

FDCPA STATEMENT: *A collection agency representative must not communicate with you at any unusual time or place or at a time or place that the collector should know would be inconvenient to you. Unless the collector has knowledge of circumstances to the contrary, he should assume that the most convenient time for contacting you is between the hours of 8 a.m. and 9 p.m.*

RESPONSE: If the collector calls you before 8 a.m. and after 9 p.m. (unless he knows you have odd working hours, such as an evening shift, or that other unusual circumstances exist), he is violating the Fair Debt Collection Practices Act. First advise the collector in writing that this is a violation; if it continues, then it can be reported to the Federal Trade Commission.

FDCPA STATEMENT: *A debt collector should not contact you at your place of employment if he knows or has reason to know that your employer prohibits such calls.*

RESPONSE: If a collector contacts you at your place of employment, you can stop the calls by sending a letter to the collection agency advising the agency employees not to contact you at work. You should send this letter certified mail, return receipt requested, so the collection agency cannot dispute having received your letter.

If you tell the collector, in writing, that you refuse to pay the debt or that you want the collector to stop calling or contacting you, the collector should not communicate with you further except to:
- advise you that it is stopping its efforts to collect the debt;
- notify you that the collector or creditor may pursue other remedies ordinarily available, such as filing a lawsuit or notifying a credit reporting agency; or,
- notify you that the collector or creditor will be taking a specific action regarding the debt, such as reporting it to the credit bureau.

FDCPA STATEMENT: *A collection agency representative must not communicate or threaten to communicate to anyone credit information about you that he knows or should know is false. If you are disputing the debt, any communication regarding the debt by the collector must also include the fact that you are disputing it.*

RESPONSE: If the collector talks to or otherwise communicates with anyone about your credit, he cannot by law give any information that he knows or should know is incorrect. If you are aware of such communication, be sure to document it in writing and notify the collector and the FTC.

FDCPA STATEMENT: *A collection agency representative must not willfully communicate with you or any member of your family so frequently as could reasonably be expected to harass you or your family, or willfully engage in other conduct that can reasonably be expected to annoy, abuse, or harass you or any member of your family.*

RESPONSE: If you get continuous telephone calls, you should keep track and write down the date and time of day for each call. To stop the continuous calls, write and send a letter to the agency, certified mail, return receipt requested, notifying the agency to stop contacting you. Once your letter is received by the agency, an agency collector is prohibited from contacting you again except to notify you that (a) contact will stop, or (b) that the agency is pursuing a specific remedy. A specific remedy might be that your debt will be assigned to a credit reporting agency.

FDCPA STATEMENT: *A collection agency representative shall not use profane, obscene, vulgar, or willfully abusive language in communicating with you or any member of your family.*

RESPONSE: If a debt collector uses profanity when calling you about payment of your debt, record the conversation, if possible, and let the collector know that the conversation is being recorded. Without the recording or some evidence of the language used, it is difficult to support your claim against the collector. You should also notify the creditor (the person to whom the debt was first owed) that the agency collector is using profanity in communications with you. The creditor might just recall your account (and other accounts) from the collection agency.

FDCPA STATEMENT: *A collection agency representative must not, in order to embarrass or disgrace you, falsely represent or imply that you have committed a crime or other misconduct.*

RESPONSE: If the collector tells you that you have committed a crime or that you are otherwise guilty of misconduct, ask him or her to explain the particular statute or law you have violated. Tell the collector that he or she should provide that information in writing. Keep track of your communication with the collector.

FDCPA STATEMENT: *A collection agency representative must not use any written communication that appears to be a legal document or that gives the appearance of being authorized, issued, or approved by a government or governmental agency, including the police, when it is not. This includes any document that looks like a court order, judgment, or a subpoena. They must not misrepresent that documents are illegal or do not require a response from you when in fact they do.*

RESPONSE: If a collection agency representative contacts you with any such type of documentation, be sure to keep a copy, then send it, along with your letter of explanation, to the FTC.

On the other hand, make sure that if you do in fact receive a legal document, you respond appropriately.

FDCPA STATEMENT: *A collection agency representative shall not communicate with you under the guise of an attorney by using the stationery of an attorney or forms or instruments that only attorneys are authorized to prepare.*

RESPONSE: A collection agency is prohibited from using a collection letter that falsely appears as though it was prepared by an attorney. A debt collector cannot send a collection letter from a legal department when no such department exists. If you have any doubt, ask to speak to the agency's attorney, and follow up with an inquiry to your local bar association. You should be able to ascertain whether or not the collection agency is trying to mislead you.

FDCPA STATEMENT: *A collection agency representative shall not orally communicate with you in such a manner as to give the false impression or appearance that it is – or is associated with – an attorney.*

RESPONSE: If a debt collector calls and even implies that it is affiliated with an attorney, ask the collector to send you a letter on the attorney's stationery. If the collector has falsely stated or implied that it is associated with an attorney, it has violated this provision. (If possible, also record the conversation for future use—after you have told the collector that the conversation is being recorded.)

FDCPA STATEMENT: *A collection agency representative must not advertise or threaten to advertise your account for sale in an effort to force you to pay, or falsely tell you that the account has been sold to a third party.*

RESPONSE: Demand that the collector provide you with written information regarding the advertisement, and/or the name and address of the party to when the account has been sold. Keep this documentation to file a complaint or lawsuit against the agency.

FDCPA STATEMENT: *A collection agency representative must not publish or post, or threaten you that he will publish or post, individual names or any list of names of consumers, commonly known as a "deadbeat list," for the purpose of enforcing or attempting to enforce collection of your debt.*

RESPONSE: Publishing your name as a debtor to force you into paying a debt is prohibited. If a collector threatens to place your name on a deadbeat list or in any manner make your debt public information, ask the collector to notify you in writing. If you receive such a letter, or have knowledge that the collector has in fact published your name, you may have a claim for damages.

FDCPA STATEMENT: *A collection agency representative must not refuse to provide adequate identification of him- or herself or employer or other entity who he or she represents when you ask him or her to do so.*

RESPONSE: A debt collector must give you his correct name and the correct name of his or her company when asked. Ask the collector to send you a statement on his or her company's letterhead containing his or her signature.

FDCPA STATEMENT: *A collection agency representative must not mail any communication to you in an envelope or post card with words typed, written, or printed on the outside of the envelope or post card calculated to embarrass you.*

RESPONSE: A debt collector is prohibited from mailing you an envelope or postcard that is intended to embarrass you into paying the debt. This includes language such as to "Deadbeat John Doe." If you receive correspondence that implies that you owe an outstanding debt, then you may have a claim for damages.

> **Example:** A woman in Utah was able to sue a collection agency for making harassing phone calls and sending a "Wanted" poster to her employer and family saying she was a "deadbeat parent" because she was behind on her child support payments.

Collectors are also prohibited from making false misrepresentations or implying that they either are, or work for, a consumer reporting agency (although some collection agencies are in fact affiliated or associated with reporting agencies).

Miscellaneous Unfair Practices

It is considered an *unfair practice* for a collector to collect or attempt to collect any amount not specifically spelled out in the agreement creating the debt.

For example, interest cannot be charged unless you initially agreed to pay it when you incurred the debt.

Accepting checks postdated more than five days is prohibited unless the collection agency notifies you no more than ten and no less than three days before that the check will be deposited.

A collection agency cannot cause you to be charged with any expenses, such as collect telephone calls, without first disclosing to you the reason for the call.

A collection agency cannot falsely threaten to take your property if it has no authority or intent to do so or if the property is exempt. (see Chapter 14.)

If You Have an Attorney

If you have employed an attorney, you must provide the collection agency with the attorney's name and address. The agency must then send all correspondence directly to the attorney and not to you.

What You Can Do on Your Own

The more knowledgeable you are about what a collection agency can and cannot do, the better equipped you will be to fight back. When contacted by a collection agency representative, keep track of the methods used to contact you, including the dates, times, and places. If at all possible, have a witness. If you believe that a collection agency has violated any of the above laws, you have several options.

You should make it clear to the collection agency representative that you are aware of the laws and believe they have been violated. You may file a lawsuit for the amount of actual damages you have suffered, and additional damages up to $1,000. In assessing your damages, the court will consider:

- the frequency and persistence of the violations by the debt collector;
- the nature of the violations; and,
- the extent to which they were intentional.

If you are successful, you will also be entitled to your court costs and attorney's fees. The collector may not be held liable if it can prove to the court that the violation was not intentional and resulted from an honest mistake.

Example: In a Texas case in 1995, a jury awarded a couple $11 million in a lawsuit against a credit card company for the abusive practices of its collection agency in attempting to collect a $2,000 debt. Collectors had made repeated phone calls and used profanity, called the debtor's office thirty-six times in one hour, threatened to disrupt the debtor's work with bomb threats, and threatened to have them killed.

In any legal action by a collection agency to collect a debt, you can use a violation of the Fair Debt Collection Practices Act as a defense.

You may file a complaint with your state Attorney General's office, or the particular government office in your state that handles collection agencies — often a consumer affairs office. (see Appendix A.) You may also register a complaint with the office of the Federal Trade Commission (FTC) nearest you. (See the sample letter on page 62.)

Finally, if you truly owe the debt and the debt collector is making legitimate, legal contact, remember that most agencies will be willing to work with you in your efforts to clear up past-due accounts. If you tell the collector that you simply are unable to pay the entire balance due, you should be able to reach an agreeable payment plan or pay a lump-sum reduced amount. Remember, it is in the agency's interest to get money in as quickly as possible. A reduced lump-sum total payment may be much more attractive than small payments extended over a long period of time.

For Further Research

The Fair Debt Collection Practices Act is found in United States Code, Title 15, Sections 1692.

Other sections of the Act include the legal actions that can be taken by debt collectors, civil liability of the collectors, and enforcement. Information can be obtained directly from the Federal Trade Commission at **www.ftc.gov**.

You should also contact your state consumer affairs office for additional information. (See Appendix A.)

Sample Letter Requesting No Contact

July 21, 2007

EZ Collections
123 Short Street
Anytown, USA

RE: Account No. 298955-3018

Dear Sir or Madam:

Please do not contact me anymore regarding the above-referenced debt.

Sincerely,
Jane Doe
CERTIFIED MAIL
RETURN RECEIPT REQUESTED
P-284-398-992

Sample Letter for Disputing a Bill

July 21, 2007

EZ Collections
123 Short Street
Anytown, USA

RE: Account No. 298955-3018

Dear Sir or Madam:

I am disputing the validity of the above-referenced debt for the following reason:
My account with Dr. Painless was paid in full on August 31, 2006.

Sincerely,
Jane Doe
CERTIFIED MAIL
RETURN RECEIPT REQUESTED
P-284-398-993

Two other examples of reasons for disputing:
"I have never had work done by ABC Drain Cleaners."
"The service provided by Mr. Smith was inadequate and not as represented by him."

Sample Letter to FTC

August 2, 2007

Federal Trade Commission
1718 Peachtree Street, NW
Room 1000
Atlanta, GA 30367

RE: EZ Collections
        123 Short Street
        Anytown, USA

Dear Sir or Madam:

On January 15, 2007, I received a letter from EZ Collections claiming I owed $50.00 to a Dr. Payne. I received a telephone call from an EZ Collections employee on April 30, 2007, demanding payment of the $50.00.

I then wrote to EZ Collections, stating that I do not know a Dr. Payne, that I was never a patient of his, and that I do not owe the $50.00.

The EZ Collections employee continued to call me and demand payment, often late at night (after 9:00 p.m.).

I am hereby making a complaint against EZ Collections for violating the Fair Debt Collection Practices Act.

Sincerely,
Jane Doe
 cc: EZ Collections

Chapter 8

The Internal Revenue Service

Unlike other creditors, the IRS has almost unlimited access to your property if you owe a tax bill. The IRS has the authority to take your house (a claim that this is your principal residence, referred to as your "homestead" under state and federal laws, does not matter), your bank accounts, your wages, your business, and virtually anything else you own in order to pay outstanding taxes. As a practical matter, most debts can be worked out with an IRS agent, and a payment plan can be arranged.

IRS Collections

As a result of Congressional hearings about the collection tactics used by some Internal Revenue Service employees, a law was passed in 1998: the *Internal Revenue Service Restructuring and Reform Act of 1998*, which has generally resulted in fewer tax audits and property seizures. The law requires an oversight board to oversee the activities of the IRS. Congress limited the use of many aggressive collection tactics and allowed taxpayers to sue examiners. Thus, collectors have in general become more accommodating and empathetic to the plight of the taxpayer.

A national taxpayer advocate was provided for to take into account the facts in a manner most favorable to the taxpayer (as opposed to the IRS). The instances in which taxpayer assistance orders are issued have been expanded to include:

- instances of immediate threat of adverse action;
- a delay of more than thirty days in solving the taxpayer's problem;

- the payment by the taxpayer of significant cost if relief is not granted; and,
- irreparable injury or tremendous long-standing adverse impact if relief is not granted.

The new law, however, does not mean that you do not have to pay taxes owed. The following pages provide general guidelines for dealing with tax payments.

Assuming Incorrect IRS Bills

If you get a notice from the IRS stating that you miscalculated your taxes due and that you still owe money, do not panic. First, check the figures. It may well be that the IRS clerk checking your return did the miscalculation. In fact, it is possible that the amount the IRS claims you owe is not actually due. During the busiest tax filing season, the IRS hires temporary workers, and many of the full-time, entry-level employees who first see your return are poorly trained. It has been estimated that nearly half of the official notices from the IRS demanding additional payments are inaccurate.

You may need help in your recalculations. If you find that the IRS has in fact made a mistake, respond to the notice, in writing, and enclose a copy of your calculations, as well as a copy of the IRS notice.

Answering an IRS Inquiry

It is of utmost importance that you respond to an IRS inquiry no later than the due date that is written on their correspondence. If you ignore the IRS letters telling you that you owe additional taxes, you will be sent:

- several statements;
- a *notice of deficiency* or a similar notice (depending upon the type of error the IRS claims you made), which gives you an opportunity to protest the IRS assessment by filing your protest in the U.S. Tax Court; and,
- an *assessment notice*, which advises you that liens are being filed against all of your property.

These liens remain until the amount due is paid. If you do not respond this time, the IRS agent may begin taking your property after a thirty-day waiting period.

Property the IRS Can Take

The IRS has the right to take virtually all of your property without any regard to the equity (except as specifically explained later in this section). The IRS agent can take your car, house, bank accounts, and wages.

The IRS can take your property, sell it for just enough to pay the taxes owed and the costs of the sale, without any consideration for the amount of equity you have in it.

Taxpayers' Bill of Rights

The Internal Revenue Service Restructuring and Reform Act of 1998 provides greater assistance to taxpayers than did the previous law. The grounds for obtaining a *Taxpayer Assistance Order* (provides relief from property seizures or collections) have been expanded. However, the list is not exclusive, and each case should be judged on its own facts. If you find yourself in such a dire situation, you may apply for such an order by filing IRS Form 911 with an IRS Problem Resolution Officer.

A list of taxpayer assistance offices can be found in the IRS publication 1546. The form is available by calling 800-829-1040 and asking for a Problem Resolution Officer to review your case. The "Taxpayer Advocate Service" can provide assistance with ongoing issues not resolved through normal procedures. This and other information about tax payments, including IRS pamphlets, is also readily available at the consumer-friendly Internal Revenue Service website at **www.irs.gov**.

What the IRS Cannot Take

There are certain items the IRS, by law, cannot touch. These are:
- clothing and school books for you or members of your family;
- fuel, food, furniture, and personal effects totalling $7,200;

- books and tools necessary for your trade, business, or profession that do not exceed $3,600 in total value;
- unemployment benefits;
- mail addressed to any person (but not yet delivered);
- certain annuity and pension payments;
- workers' compensation benefits;
- judgments for support of minor children (if you have been ordered to pay, the amount necessary for you to comply with judgment is exempt);
- minimum exemption for wages, salary, and other income;
- certain service-connected disability payments;
- certain public assistance payments; and,
- assistance under the *Job Training Partnership Act.*

Your primary residence may be exempt, *unless* the district or assistant district IRS director approves the levy on your property or the secretary of the IRS finds that collection of the tax is in jeopardy.

IRS Time Limitations

The IRS can come after you for additional taxes only three years after you filed the return. However, if the IRS finds that the gross income shown on your return was 25% less than the actual amount, the time limitation is increased to six years. If you failed to file or filed a fraudulent return, there is no time limitation. The collection process is described in detail in IRS Publication No. 594.

Audits

Every year, a certain number of tax returns are chosen by the IRS for an audit. An *audit* simply means an official examination and verification of your financial accounts and records. A return may be selected for audit because of certain information it contains — such as deductions for home office expenses — or it may be a random selection. Audits are made by correspondence (you are asked to send in supporting evidence of figures), in an IRS examiner's office, or at your home or office.

To prepare for an audit of your tax return, you should make sure that all your records are in order and that the figures on your tax return can be supported by documentation. In other words, if you have deducted costs for entertainment as a business expense, you should be able to clearly show the IRS examiner that the entertainment was in fact for a business purpose. Similarly, if you have deducted expenses for maintaining a portion of your home as an office, be able to show that the area is being used exclusively for your business.

Representation

You may want to have someone represent you at the audit—an accountant, your bookkeeper, or in some cases, an attorney—removing you from the immediate scrutiny and questioning of the examiner. You do not have to be physically present at the audit. Your representative can come back to you for clarification of any items questioned by the examiner and give you an opportunity to put some forethought into your response. If you do go alone and questions come up that you are unable to answer adequately, then you can tell the examiner that you will have to consult with your accountant or other tax advisor.

Preparation

Although the majority of audits result in the taxpayer owing money, it is not always the case. The important point to remember is to be prepared. Of course, preparation should begin long before you receive notice of an audit. Keep accurate records throughout each year that support the figures on your return, and your audit should go smoothly. Finally, if the examiner's report shows that you owe additional tax, you will have thirty days to accept or contest the decision.

What You Can Do

The first step, of course, is to file your tax returns (or request for extensions), on or before the IRS deadline. If you are charged a penalty for filing late, send a notarized statement and whatever documentation you have showing the date it was mailed. If you are filing late, include a letter and available supporting evidence explaining why. The IRS examiner may accept the late filing without a penalty.

Even if you have met the deadlines, it may not be enough. The IRS can come back to you for more money. This is done by sending you a letter stating that there is a deficiency in your tax payment.

- If you dispute a calculation, send a letter of explanation, including your calculation. Keep your letter short, simple, and to the point so it can be easily understood. (See page 70 for a sample letter.) The IRS notices usually come in duplicate, giving you the copy to use for your response. You should include this copy, and always reference the IRS file number on your correspondence to make sure it does not get lost. You should send correspondence by certified mail, with a return receipt requested. This way, there can be no dispute by the IRS that they received your response.

- If you get further notices without any acknowledgment of the letter you sent, write again and include copies of all correspondence you already sent regarding that particular claim. If you still get another notice, contact the IRS Problem Resolution Officer nearest you. If you believe the IRS is beyond the time limitation, you can file a petition in the U.S. Tax Court to have the taxes, interest, and penalties dropped. (See page 71 for a sample petition.)

- If you owe the bill, negotiate with the IRS for a reduced lump-sum amount or arrange a payment plan. If you do set up a payment plan, make sure you keep the payments current. If you do not, the IRS can take other actions to collect.

- Consider taking out a loan from your bank or other source, if possible, and paying the IRS off. It may be better to owe money to the bank than to risk your house being seized by the IRS. This would also eliminate the IRS charging for penalties and interest. (If the IRS has waived penalties, or none are being charged, then a payment plan with the IRS might make better economic sense.)

- Finally, a bankruptcy filing will temporarily stop all actions by the IRS to collect unpaid taxes. However, bankruptcy will not discharge your debt to the IRS (unless the time limitation has expired and you have not had negotiations with the IRS or a tax court case determination within 240 days of filing the bankruptcy petition). A Chapter 13 filing will not discharge the debt for unpaid taxes, but will allow you to pay the entire amount due according to your repayment plan schedule set up through the bankruptcy procedure.

For Further Research

The IRS list of exemptions is found in United States Code Title 12, Chapter 64, Subtitle F-Collection, Section 6334. A list of IRS publications is available at **www.irs.gov/formspubs/index.html**.

The text of these publications is available either by mail or directly on the website. IRS Publication 1 explains your rights as a taxpayer, including your rights to taxpayer assistance.

The Internal Revenue Service also provides information by telephone (800-829-1040), and forms by calling 800-829-3676. The general website is **www.irs.gov**.

Sample Letter to IRS

September 20, 2007

Internal Revenue Service
Atlanta, GA 39901

RE: Jane Doe
Social Security No. 555-55-5555
Your file reference no. 95-34453

Dear Sir or Madam,

I have received your letter of September 10, 2007, a copy of which is attached, advising me that I still owe $759.28.

I have recalculated my 2006 tax return and came up with the same figures as before. My calculations are attached.

Please correct your records and stop sending me notices, or explain specifically where and how the error is to be found. Thank you.

Sincerely,
Jane Doe
CERTIFIED MAIL
RETURN RECEIPT REQUESTED
P-288-398-487

This letter should be sent in response to a notice of deficiency or a correction notice.

Sample Tax Case Petition Form

PETITION
(SMALL TAX CASE)
UNITED STATES TAX COURT

Jane Doe,	)
Petitioner,	)
	)
vs.	) Docket No. 55555
	)
Commissioner of Internal Revenue,	)
Respondent.	)

PETITION

1. Petitioner asks the Court to redetermine the tax deficiencies for the year 2006 as set forth in the Notice of Deficiency dated September 10, 2007, a copy of which is attached to this Petition. The Notice was issued by the Office of the Internal Revenue Service at Atlanta, Georgia.

2. Petitioner's taxpayer identification number (Social Security number) is 555-55-5555.

3. Petitioner makes the following claim(s) regarding his/their tax liability:

Year	Amount of Deficiency Disputed	Addition to Tax (Penalty) Disputed	Amount of Over-payment Claim
2006	$759.28	$113.90	-0-

4. Those adjustments or changes in the Notice of Deficiency with which Petitioners disagrees and why: the IRS has failed to show where any errors were made in the Petitioner's tax return as originally filed.

Petitioner requests that the proceedings in this case be conducted as a "Small Tax Case" under Section 7463 of the Internal Revenue Code of 1954, as amended, and Rule 172 of the Rules of Practice and Procedure of the United States Tax Court. A decision in a "Small Tax Case" is final and cannot be appealed by either party.

Jane Doe
_____
Signature of Petitioner
447 Tea Party Lane
Clearwater, FL 33760
(813) 555-555

Chapter 9

Loan Disclosure Requirements — Truth in Lending

Although the text of the federal *Consumer Credit Act*, which includes the *Consumer Credit Cost Disclosure Requirements*, is too extensive and complex to recite in this book, it is important for you to know that you have the right to certain information about a loan given to you by a lender or creditor.

The Federal Law

Congress established the *cost disclosure requirements* to assure that every creditor who, in the ordinary course of business, regularly extends, offers to extend, or arranges for the extension of consumer credit, gives meaningful information regarding the cost of the credit and other relevant information. This is so that you may readily compare the various credit terms available to you from different sources and avoid the uninformed use of credit.

You should have the benefit of sufficient information about the proposed loan so that you can make an informed decision as to whether you want to accept the terms. If you have not had the benefit of all the information that the law requires the creditor give you, then you may have the basis for a lawsuit against the creditor. Or, you may have a counterclaim if the creditor sues you for nonpayment.

The *Truth in Lending* regulations (also known as *Regulation Z* or *Reg Z*), set forth the rules with which lenders must comply when they give you credit. (C.F.R., Title 12, Chapter II, Part 226.) It gives you the right to cancel certain credit transactions that involve a lien on your residence. It also gives you certain legal rights if the lender has misrepresented a loan to you, or has failed to make all the disclosures accurately as required under the law. (The Consumer Credit Act requires disclosure in other consumer credit transactions, as well as leases and credit cards. These are discussed in Chapters 10 and 11.)

Required Disclosures
The disclosures that must be made by a lender include:
- the identity of the creditor (lender);
- the amount financed, which is the amount of credit of which the borrower has actual use;
- along with the disclosure of the amount financed, a statement of your right to obtain, upon a written request, a written itemization of the amount financed (which must then be furnished);
- the finance charge;
- the finance charge expressed as an annual percentage rate;
- the number, amount, and due dates or period of payments scheduled to repay the total loan;
- (where the lender is also the seller), the total of the cash price of the property and the finance charge;
- descriptive explanations of the terms:
  - amount financed,
  - finance charge,
  - annual percentage rate,
  - total of payments, and,
  - total sale price;

  NOTE: *The descriptive explanation of total sale price must include a reference to the amount of the down payment;*

- where credit is secured, as with a mortgage, a statement that a security interest has been taken in either (a) the property that is purchased as part of the credit transaction, or (b) property not purchased as part of the credit transaction identified by item or type;

- any dollar charge or percentage amount that may be imposed by a creditor solely on account of a late payment, other than a deferment or extension charge;
- a statement as to whether or not you are entitled to a rebate of any finance charge upon refinancing or prepayment in full, if the obligation involves a precomputed finance charge. A statement as to whether or not there will be a penalty imposed in those same circumstances if the obligation involves a finance charge computed from time to time by application of a rate to the unpaid principal balance;
- a statement that you should refer to the appropriate contract document for any information that document provides about nonpayment, default, the right to accelerate the maturity of the debt, and prepayment rebates and penalties;
- in any residential mortgage transaction, a statement indicating whether someone who buys the property from you may assume the debt obligation on its original terms and conditions;
- any variable rate information;
- information about a demand feature of the financing (when payment can be demanded by creditor);
- creditor's late payment policy;
- information about any security interest the creditor is taking and related charges;
- insurance requirements; and,
- required deposit information.

Errors by the creditor in the Truth in Lending Disclosures are usually not brought to the creditor's attention by the borrower until the creditor tries to collect the debt. If the creditor finds an error before any default in payment, the creditor will probably prepare new documents with the correct information.

Time Periods in which Disclosures Must be Made

Lenders are required to provide you with specific information about the terms of financing within certain prescribed time periods, as follows.

Telephone Orders

You may place a purchase order by mail or telephone without being personally solicited by the creditor. The cash price, total sale price, and the terms of financing, including the annual percentage rate, are set forth in the creditor's catalog or other printed material distributed to the public. The required disclosures may be made by the creditor at any time earlier than the first payment due date.

Loan Requests by Telephone

You may make a request for a loan by mail or telephone even when the creditor has not personally solicited you. The terms of financing, including the annual percentage rate for representative amounts of credit, are set forth in the creditor's printed material distributed to the public, in the loan contract, or other printed material delivered to you. Then, the disclosures must be made no later than the date the first payment is due.

If the creditor personally solicits you in either case, the disclosures must be made *before* you obligate yourself to the creditor.

Purchasing in a Series

Your purchase may be one of a series according to an agreement providing that the deferred payment price of a particular sale be added to the existing outstanding balance. If you have already agreed to the annual percentage rate and finance charge, and the creditor is not retaining a security interest in any of the property you have purchased, then the disclosure may be made any time before the first payment is due.

NOTE: *See also "Good Faith Estimate – Residential Mortgages" on page 81.*

Finance Charge and Annual Percentage Rate (APR)

Regulation Z spells out exactly how the finance charge and annual percentage rate on your loan are to be determined, and how these and other charges related to your loan are to be disclosed to you. The manner in which these calculations are made is determined by federal statute and by the Board of Governors of the Federal Reserve System (Board).

Finance Charge

In determining whether a lender has given you all the required information about your loan, one of the most important items to review is the finance charge. The *finance charge* is determined as the sum of all charges, payable directly or indirectly by the borrower, and imposed directly or indirectly by the creditor as an incident to the extension of credit. The following charges are examples of costs included in the finance charge:

- interest and any amount payable under a point, discount, or other system of additional charges;
- service or carrying charge;
- loan fee, finder's fee, or similar charge;
- fee for an investigation or credit report; or,
- premium or other charge for any guarantee or insurance protecting the creditor against the obligor's default or other credit loss.

> **Example:** A buyer of a food freezer was required to purchase a freezer service policy to assure repair of the freezer for the duration of the period the buyer agreed to make installment payments. The charge for the service policy was added to the sale price and included in the amount financed, but not disclosed to the buyer. The cost of the freezer service policy was a finance charge, the disclosure of which was required by law. The seller was liable for damages to the buyer.

In deciding whether an item must be included in the finance charge, the important question is whether the lender refuses to extend credit until you agree to pay the charge. If a charge is not itemized and disclosed by the lender, it still needs to be included in the computation of the finance charge, even if the charge is not a charge for credit.

Annual Percentage Rate (APR)

The *Annual Percentage Rate* (APR) simply reflects the cost of your loan as a yearly rate. This figure must be disclosed to you, because it will usually be higher than the interest rate you are paying on your note. Borrowers often wonder whether the bank has increased the interest rate quoted to them. The difference between the interest rate quoted and stated on your promissory note and the interest rate (APR) shown on the disclosure form is due to difference in calculations.

There are several methods of determining the annual percentage rate applied to your loan. The most important point to remember is that any prepaid finance charges are considered a reduction in the *principal* amount of the loan.

> **Example:** If you borrow $10,000 at 10% interest for one year, the bank deducts $300 in loan closing costs from the $10,000, and you must make up the difference, then you have actually only received $9,700. The total of 10% interest on $10,000, or $1,000, is $11,000. This is the amount you will pay according to your loan. However, because of the deduction of closing costs, the bank is actually giving you only $9,700. The total of $11,000 you will pay ($10,000 plus $1,000 interest) is actually $9,700 (the $10,000 less $300 in charges) at 13.40% interest.

Remember that any income the bank earns as the result of your loan is considered a finance charge, including a bank appraisal fee, document preparation fee, points, origination fee, etc. These charges should be considered a reduction in the principal amount of the loan.

The lender will take three variables into consideration in computing the APR:

1. the number of payments to be made over the complete term of the loan (usually 360 for a real estate loan);

2. the interest rate; and,

3. the principal balance remaining to be paid on the loan after deducting those items that are prepaid finance charges.

The fourth variable, the total of the periodic (monthly) payments (principal and interest), will then be computed. This is a complicated calculation, and should be reviewed by someone competent and experienced in applying the Regulation Z requirements. A rough approximation of the calculation is as follows:

- first, the finance charge to be paid over the term of the loan is totalled (in a real estate loan, the monthly finance charge will vary according to an amortization schedule);
- second, this total is then divided by the number of years of the loan; and,
- third, this figure is again divided by the total amount financed (including the principal amount of the loan and reflecting any finance charges).

NOTE: *An APR on an open-end (equity line) loan is calculated as if the loan were carried out to full term at the highest interest rate.*

All items required to be disclosed must be disclosed clearly, conspicuously, and in meaningful sequence. The terms *annual percentage rate* and *finance charge* must be disclosed more conspicuously than other terms or information provided in connection with a transaction, except information relating the identity of the creditor. The disclosures must be made to the person who is to be obligated on the loan. (If you are taking out the loan with your father's advice, then the disclosures must be made to you—making them to your father is not sufficient.)

Truth in Lending Disclosure Statement

A sample *Truth in Lending Disclosure Statement* is on page 94. The box titled Annual Percentage Rate may be different from the rate quoted to you at the time of your mortgage application, and may be different from the interest rate you were promised. This rate should reflect any prepaid costs or items included in the financing.

Example: The rate shown is 9.65%. The rate the borrower is paying on an $80,000 loan is 9.25%. The promissory note will show $80,000 to be paid back at 9.25% interest. Take the $80,000, less $2,728 in total closing costs (which includes $800 origination fee, $1600 discount points, $113 appraisal fee, $50 credit report, and $165 underwriting fee). The $77,272, with the payments calculated on the $80,000 amount (since $80,000 includes the amount paid on behalf of and given to the borrower), comes to 9.65% annual percentage rate.

The box titled *Finance Charge* shows the total amount of interest you will be paying over the total term of the loan.

The box titled *Amount Financed* is somewhat less than the amount of the mortgage because the prepaid costs have been deducted, as described above.

The box titled *Total of Payments* is the total of the figures in the previous two boxes, representing the total amount that you will be paying if you pay the full term of the loan.

NOTE: *Although beyond the scope of this book, you should also be sure that banks and other real estate lenders are required to follow the federal Real Estate Settlement Procedures Act of 1974 (RESPA), which regulates settlement of a residential loan transaction. For information about RESPA, write to:*

U.S. Department of Housing and Urban Development
Director, Office of Insured Single Family Housing
Attention: RESPA
451 Seventh Street, SW
Washington, DC 20410
202-708-1112

At **www.hud.gov**, detailed information about the disclosure requirements is available.

For information regarding manufactured home financing requirements, contact:

Office of Manufactured Housing and Regulatory Functions
451 Seventh Street, SW
Washington, DC 20410

Good Faith Estimate—Residential Mortgages

In a residential mortgage transaction, the lender must make a *good faith* (reasonable and as accurate as possible) estimate of the disclosures required under Regulation Z *before* the credit is extended, or the lender must either deliver or place the estimate in the mail to the borrower *no later than three business days* after the lender receives the borrower's written application, whichever date is earlier. If the good faith estimate contains an annual percentage rate that is subsequently determined to be inaccurate by the acceptable calculations, then the lender must furnish another good faith estimate at the time of settlement (when the loan is actually made and documents signed). (See page 95 for a sample good faith estimate.)

Equity Line Mortgages and Your Right to Rescind

If you have borrowed funds for purposes other than the purchase of your principal residence, and the lender has taken an interest in your residence as collateral for the loan, the law requires that you be given a three-day *right of rescission*. In other words, you have until midnight of the third business day, following the date of signing the loan documents or receipt of all the required disclosures, to cancel the loan. However, you must notify the creditor by mail, telegram, or other writing of your cancellation.

Every joint owner who will be obligated to pay back the loan has the right to receive the disclosures and must be given a notice of the right to cancel. (See page 97 for a sample notice.)

Release from Your Obligations

When you exercise your right to rescind, you are not liable for any finance or other charge. Any security interest the creditor may have in your property becomes void. Within twenty days after you exercise your right to rescind, the creditor must return to you any money or property given as earnest money, down payment, or otherwise, and must take any action required to reflect the termination of any security interest the creditor may have acquired as a result of the transaction.

Property to Be Returned to Creditor

As the borrower you must also return to the creditor, within a reasonable time period after you rescind the transaction, any funds or value the creditor has advanced to you. However, if the creditor fails to return the property required to be returned to you, then you have no further obligation to return the funds to the creditor.

If the Creditor Fails to Take the Property

If the creditor does not take possession of the property within ten days of the date you offer, you may be entitled to keep the property. (In most cases, this would involve a return of the principal amount loaned to you by the creditor.) A court can refuse your request to have the transaction rescinded if you fail to return any loan proceeds advanced to you by the lender.

Loans Not Affected by Right of Rescission

The right of rescission does not apply to:
- a *residential mortgage transaction* when the funds are used to purchase the property;
- a transaction that constitutes the refinancing or consolidation (with no new advances) of the principal balance then due and any accrued and unpaid finance charges of an existing extension of credit by the same creditor, secured by an interest in the same property;

- a transaction when an agency of a state is a creditor; or,
- advances under a preexisting open-end credit plan if a security interest has already been retained or acquired by the lender and such advances are in accordance with a previously established credit limit for such plan.

If the lender fails to provide you with the information required to be disclosed, you have three years from the date of the conclusion of the transaction, or when you sell the property, whichever comes first, to rescind the transaction. If the creditor fails to disclose required information, you are not limited by the normal three-day rescission period.

Balloon Payments on Consumer Loans

Some states prohibit *balloon payments* on consumer loans for family or household purposes; others require that you be given the right to refinance the loan when the balloon payment comes due. (A *balloon payment* is the amount due at the end of a loan term after you have made regular, smaller payments for a period of time.) Your state attorney general's office or the consumer office should have information regarding balloon payments on consumer loans.

Refinancing

If any existing extension of credit is refinanced, two or more existing extensions of credit are consolidated, or an existing obligation is increased, these will be considered new transactions subject to the disclosure requirements of the Act. If your loan has been refinanced or the terms have otherwise changed, determine whether your lender gave you all the required information.

When Disclosure Is Not Required

The disclosure requirements described above do not apply to the following transactions:

- credit transactions involving extensions of credit primarily for business, commercial, or agricultural purposes, or to government or governmental agencies, or to organizations;
- transactions in securities or commodities accounts by a broker-dealer registered with the Securities and Exchange Commission (SEC);
- credit transactions, other than those in which a security interest is or will be acquired in *real property*, or in *personal property* used or expected to be used as the principal dwelling of the consumer, in which the total amount financed exceeds $25,000; or,
- transactions under public utility tariffs, if the Board determines that a state regulatory body regulates the charges for the public utility services involved, the charges for delayed payment, and any discount allowed for early payment.

The numerous laws and regulations under the Consumer Credit Act cover consumer credit transactions primarily for personal, family, household, or agricultural purposes.

Lenders' Liabilities and Your Rights and Obligations

The creditor has no liability if, within sixty days of discovering an error and before receiving notice from you of the error, the creditor notifies you and makes the appropriate adjustments. The creditor makes sure that you will not be required to pay an amount greater than the charge actually disclosed, or the dollar equivalent of the annual percentage rate actually disclosed, whichever is lower.

The creditor will not be held liable if the creditor shows that the violation was not intentional and resulted from an honest error, including clerical or computer malfunction. However, an error of legal judgment with respect to a person's obligations is not considered an honest error. In most real estate loan transactions with a commercial lender, you will be asked to sign a document that says you agree to cooperate if a correction is required due to a clerical error. (See page 96 for a sample compliance agreement.)

You have no legal right to offset any amount that the creditor may owe you against any other amount you owe the creditor, unless you have a court judgment against the creditor. However, you should assert the creditor's violation of the Consumer Credit Act as a defense against any legal action to collect a debt brought by a creditor who is in violation of the Act.

NOTE: *In a real estate foreclosure action, Regulation Z may be your strongest defense.*

Considering the volume of paperwork required in a loan transaction and the number of transactions a commercial lender may make, it is possible that an error was made. You should get a copy of all the disclosure documents related to your loan. You should then review them carefully with someone who fully understands the disclosure requirements and the calculations. If there is a possibility of an error, it may be wise for you to hire an attorney to review the documents and give you an opinion as to whether you should proceed legally against the lender. (Even if ultimately the court does not agree that the lender violated the Consumer Credit Act, using this as a defense will delay the lender's lawsuit, including a foreclosure action.)

NOTE: *If you are successful in a lawsuit against a creditor who violated any provisions of the Consumer Credit Act, your attorney's fees and costs must be paid by the creditor.*

For any violation of the Consumer Credit Act, a creditor may be liable to you in an amount equal to:
- any actual damage suffered by you as a result of the failure to disclose all of the information required;
- twice the amount of any finance charge in connection with the transaction; or,
- the reasonable attorney's fees and costs incurred in a successful legal action.

Credit Application Worksheet

The questions on pages 87–89 are typical of what you will find on an application form, whether for a credit card or other consumer loan. Before approaching a lender, you may want to complete this form, so you will have the information readily available when asked.

For Further Research

If you need additional information regarding Regulation Z, mortgage settlement costs, credit protection laws, etc., you may write to:

Division of Consumer and Community Affairs
Board of Governors of the Federal Reserve System
20ᵗʰ Street and Constitution Ave NW
Washington, DC 20551
www.federalreserve.gov

You may also write to your regional Federal Trade Commission office, Division of Credit Practices, Bureau of Consumer Affairs. (see Appendix B.) The text of the Act is contained in United States Code, Title 15, Chapter 41, Subchapter I, Consumer Credit Cost Disclosure, Sections 1601 through 1635. The regulations enforcing the laws are found in the Code of Federal Regulations, Title 12, Banks & Banking, Part 226, Truth in Lending (Regulation Z).

Sample Loan Application Form

AMOUNT REQUESTED:

FOR HOW LONG: _____

LOAN PROCEEDS TO BE USED FOR: _____

LAST NAME: _____

FIRST NAME: _____

ADDRESS: _____

_____

IF LESS THAN THREE YEARS AT THIS ADDRESS, GIVE
PREVIOUS ADDRESS:

_____

_____

TELEPHONE NUMBER_____

SOCIAL SECURITY NUMBER: _____

SPOUSE'S (IF ANY) NAME AND SOCIAL SECURITY NUMBER:

_____

_____

NUMBER OF DEPENDENTS: _____

CURRENT EMPLOYER'S NAME AND ADDRESS:

_____

_____

DATE EMPLOYED: _____

OCCUPATION: _____

IF LESS THAN THREE YEARS WITH THE ABOVE EMPLOYER,
GIVE NAME AND ADDRESS OF PREVIOUS EMPLOYER:

_____

_____

DATES EMPLOYED: _____

CURRENT SALARY: _____

OTHER INCOME: (LIST SOURCES AND AMOUNTS)

_____

_____

LIST ASSETS:
REAL ESTATE OWNED (LOCATION & CURRENT VALUE):

_____

_____

_____

VEHICLES (MAKE AND YEAR):

_____

_____

OTHER ASSETS (CERTIFICATES OF DEPOSITS, SAVINGS ACCOUNTS, STOCKS, LIFE INSURANCE, ETC.—GIVE DESCRIPTION AND CURRENT VALUES)

_____

_____

_____

LIABILITIES (MORTGAGES, AUTO LOANS, LEASES, CONSUMER LOANS, ALIMONY OR SUPPORT, ETC.—LIST ORIGINAL AMOUNT AND CURRENT BALANCE OWING):

_____

_____

_____

LIST MONTHLY LOAN OBLIGATIONS
(PAYEE AND MONTHLY PAYMENT AMOUNT):

_____

_____

_____

MONTHLY RENT PAYMENT (IF APPLICABLE):

_____

HAVE YOU FILED FOR OR BEEN DISCHARGED IN BANKRUPTCY DURING THE PAST TEN YEARS? YES OR NO _____
IF YES, WHERE? _____
ARE YOU A GUARANTOR OR JOINTLY LIABLE ON ANY LOAN OR CONTRACT? YES OR NO _____

IF SO, DESCRIBE OBLIGATION AND AMOUNT:

_____

_____

_____

ARE THERE ANY OUTSTANDING JUDGMENTS AGAINST YOU?
YES OR NO _____

IF SO, DESCRIBE CIRCUMSTANCES AND AMOUNT:

_____

_____

_____

SIGNATURE: _____

DATE: _____

Sample Uniform Residential Loan Application

Uniform Residential Loan Application

This application is designed to be completed by the applicant(s) with the Lender's assistance. Applicants should complete this form as "Borrower" or "Co-Borrower," as applicable. Co-Borrower information must also be provided (and the appropriate box checked) when ☐ the income or assets of a person other than the "Borrower" (including the Borrower's spouse) will be used as a basis for loan qualification or ☐ the income or assets of the Borrower's spouse will not be used as a basis for loan qualification, but his or her liabilities must be considered because the Borrower resides in a community property state, the security property is located in a community property state, or the Borrower is relying on other property located in a community property state as a basis for repayment of the loan.

I. TYPE OF MORTGAGE AND TERMS OF LOAN

Mortgage Applied for:	☐ VA ☐ FHA	☐ Conventional ☐ USDA/Rural Housing Service	☐ Other (explain):	Agency Case Number	Lender Case Number

Amount $	Interest Rate %	No. of Months	Amortization Type:	☐ Fixed Rate ☐ GPM	☐ Other (explain): ☐ ARM (type):

II. PROPERTY INFORMATION AND PURPOSE OF LOAN

Subject Property Address (street, city, state, & ZIP)	No. of Units

Legal Description of Subject Property (attach description if necessary)	Year Built

Purpose of Loan ☐ Purchase ☐ Construction ☐ Refinance ☐ Construction-Permanent	☐ Other (explain):	Property will be: ☐ Primary Residence ☐ Secondary Residence ☐ Investment

Complete this line if construction or construction-permanent loan.

Year Lot Acquired	Original Cost	Amount Existing Liens	(a) Present Value of Lot	(b) Cost of Improvements	Total (a + b)
	$	$	$	$	$

Complete this line if this is a refinance loan.

Year Acquired	Original Cost	Amount Existing Liens	Purpose of Refinance	Describe Improvements ☐ made ☐ to be made
	$	$		Cost: $

Title will be held in what Name(s)	Manner in which Title will be held	Estate will be held in: ☐ Fee Simple ☐ Leasehold (show expiration date)

Source of Down Payment, Settlement Charges and/or Subordinate Financing (explain)	

III. BORROWER INFORMATION

Borrower	Co-Borrower
Borrower's Name (include Jr. or Sr. if applicable)	Co-Borrower's Name (include Jr. or Sr. if applicable)

Social Security Number	Home Phone (incl. area code)	DOB (MM/DD/YYYY)	Yrs. School	Social Security Number	Home Phone (incl. area code)	DOB (MM/DD/YYYY)	Yrs. School

☐ Married ☐ Unmarried (include single, ☐ Separated divorced, widowed)	Dependents (not listed by Co-Borrower) no. ages	☐ Married ☐ Unmarried (include single, ☐ Separated divorced, widowed)	Dependents (not listed by Borrower) no. ages

Present Address (street, city, state, ZIP) ☐ Own ☐ Rent _____No. Yrs.	Present Address (street, city, state, ZIP) ☐ Own ☐ Rent _____No. Yrs.

Mailing Address, if different from Present Address	Mailing Address, if different from Present Address

If residing at present address for less than two years, complete the following:

Former Address (street, city, state, ZIP) ☐ Own ☐ Rent _____No. Yrs.	Former Address (street, city, state, ZIP) ☐ Own ☐ Rent _____No. Yrs.

IV. EMPLOYMENT INFORMATION

Borrower		Co-Borrower	
Name & Address of Employer	☐ Self Employed	Yrs. on this job	Name & Address of Employer	☐ Self Employed	Yrs. on this job
		Yrs. employed in this line of work/profession			Yrs. employed in this line of work/profession
Position/Title/Type of Business		Business Phone (incl. area code)	Position/Title/Type of Business		Business Phone (incl. area code)

If employed in current position for less than two years or if currently employed in more than one position, complete the following:

Name & Address of Employer	☐ Self Employed	Dates (from – to)	Name & Address of Employer	☐ Self Employed	Dates (from – to)
		Monthly Income $			Monthly Income $
Position/Title/Type of Business		Business Phone (incl. area code)	Position/Title/Type of Business		Business Phone (incl. area code)

Name & Address of Employer	☐ Self Employed	Dates (from – to)	Name & Address of Employer	☐ Self Employed	Dates (from – to)
		Monthly Income $			Monthly Income $
Position/Title/Type of Business		Business Phone (incl. area code)	Position/Title/Type of Business		Business Phone (incl. area code)

V. MONTHLY INCOME AND COMBINED HOUSING EXPENSE INFORMATION

Gross Monthly Income	Borrower	Co-Borrower	Total	Combined Monthly Housing Expense	Present	Proposed
Base Empl. Income*	$	$	$	Rent	$	
Overtime				First Mortgage (P&I)		$
Bonuses				Other Financing (P&I)		
Commissions				Hazard Insurance		
Dividends/Interest				Real Estate Taxes		
Net Rental Income				Mortgage Insurance		
Other (before completing, see the notice in "describe other income," below)				Homeowner Assn. Dues		
				Other:		
Total	$	$	$	Total	$	$

* Self Employed Borrower(s) may be required to provide additional documentation such as tax returns and financial statements.

Describe Other Income *Notice:* Alimony, child support, or separate maintenance income need not be revealed if the Borrower (B) or Co-Borrower (C) does not choose to have it considered for repaying this loan.

B/C		Monthly Amount
		$

VI. ASSETS AND LIABILITIES

This Statement and any applicable supporting schedules may be completed jointly by both married and unmarried Co-Borrowers if their assets and liabilities are sufficiently joined so that the Statement can be meaningfully and fairly presented on a combined basis; otherwise, separate Statements and Schedules are required. If the Co-Borrower section was completed about a spouse, this Statement and supporting schedules must be completed about that spouse also.

Completed ☐ Jointly ☐ Not Jointly

ASSETS Description	Cash or Market Value	Liabilities and Pledged Assets. List the creditor's name, address and account number for all outstanding debts, including automobile loans, revolving charge accounts, real estate loans, alimony, child support, stock pledges, etc. Use continuation sheet, if necessary. Indicate by (*) those liabilities which will be satisfied upon sale of real estate owned or upon refinancing of the subject property.		
Cash deposit toward purchase held by:	$			
		LIABILITIES	Monthly Payment & Months Left to Pay	Unpaid Balance
List checking and savings accounts below		Name and address of Company	$ Payment/Months	$
Name and address of Bank, S&L, or Credit Union				
		Acct. no.		
Acct. no.	$	Name and address of Company	$ Payment/Months	$
Name and address of Bank, S&L, or Credit Union				
		Acct. no.		
Acct. no.	$	Name and address of Company	$ Payment/Months	$
Name and address of Bank, S&L, or Credit Union				
		Acct. no.		
Acct. no.	$	Name and address of Company	$ Payment/Months	$
Name and address of Bank, S&L, or Credit Union				
		Acct. no.		
Acct. no.	$	Name and address of Company	$ Payment/Months	$
Stocks & Bonds (Company name/number & description)	$			
		Acct. no.		
		Name and address of Company	$ Payment/Months	$
Life insurance net cash value	$			
Face amount: $				
Subtotal Liquid Assets	$			
Real estate owned (enter market value from schedule of real estate owned)	$	Acct. no.		
		Name and address of Company	$ Payment/Months	$
Vested interest in retirement fund	$			
Net worth of business(es) owned (attach financial statement)	$			
Automobiles owned (make and year)	$	Acct. no.		
		Alimony/Child Support/Separate Maintenance Payments Owed to:	$	
Other Assets (itemize)	$	Job-Related Expense (child care, union dues, etc.)	$	
		Total Monthly Payments	$	
Total Assets a.	$	Net Worth (a minus b) ▶ $	Total Liabilities b.	$

VI. ASSETS AND LIABILITIES (cont.)

Schedule of Real Estate Owned (If additional properties are owned, use continuation sheet.)

Property Address (enter S if sold, PS if pending sale or R if rental being held for income)	Type of Property	Present Market Value	Amount of Mortgages & Liens	Gross Rental Income	Mortgage Payments	Insurance, Maintenance, Taxes & Misc.	Net Rental Income
		$	$	$	$	$	$
	Totals $	$	$	$	$	$	$

List any additional names under which credit has previously been received and indicate appropriate creditor name(s) and account number(s):

Alternate Name	Creditor Name	Account Number

VII. DETAILS OF TRANSACTION | VIII. DECLARATIONS

					Borrower		Co-Borrower	
			If you answer "Yes" to any questions a through i, please use continuation sheet for explanation.		Yes	No	Yes	No
a.	Purchase price	$						
b.	Alterations, improvements, repairs		a. Are there any outstanding judgments against you?		❑	❑	❑	❑
c.	Land (if acquired separately)		b. Have you been declared bankrupt within the past 7 years?		❑	❑	❑	❑
d.	Refinance (incl. debts to be paid off)		c. Have you had property foreclosed upon or given title or deed in lieu thereof in the last 7 years?		❑	❑	❑	❑
e.	Estimated prepaid items							
f.	Estimated closing costs		d. Are you a party to a lawsuit?		❑	❑	❑	❑
g.	PMI, MIP, Funding Fee		e. Have you directly or indirectly been obligated on any loan which resulted in foreclosure, transfer of title in lieu of foreclosure, or judgment?		❑	❑	❑	❑
h.	Discount (if Borrower will pay)		(This would include such loans as home mortgage loans, SBA loans, home improvement loans, educational loans, manufactured (mobile) home loans, any mortgage, financial obligation, bond, or loan guarantee. If "Yes," provide details, including date, name and address of Lender, FHA or VA case number, if any, and reasons for the action.)					
i.	**Total costs (add items a through h)**							
j.	Subordinate financing							
k.	Borrower's closing costs paid by Seller		f. Are you presently delinquent or in default on any Federal debt or any other loan, mortgage, financial obligation, bond, or loan guarantee? If "Yes," give details as described in the preceding question.		❑	❑	❑	❑
l.	Other Credits (explain)		g. Are you obligated to pay alimony, child support, or separate maintenance?		❑	❑	❑	❑
m.	Loan amount (exclude PMI, MIP, Funding Fee financed)		h. Is any part of the down payment borrowed?		❑	❑	❑	❑
			i. Are you a co-maker or endorser on a note?		❑	❑	❑	❑
n.	PMI, MIP, Funding Fee financed		j. Are you a U.S. citizen?		❑	❑	❑	❑
			k. Are you a permanent resident alien?		❑	❑	❑	❑
o.	Loan amount (add m & n)		l. Do you intend to occupy the property as your primary residence? If "Yes," complete question m below.		❑	❑	❑	❑
			m. Have you had an ownership interest in a property in the last three years?		❑	❑	❑	❑
p.	Cash from/to Borrower (subtract j, k, l & o from i)		(1) What type of property did you own—principal residence (PR), second home (SH), or investment property (IP)?					
			(2) How did you hold title to the home—by yourself (S), jointly with your spouse (SP), or jointly with another person (O)?					

IX. ACKNOWLEDGMENT AND AGREEMENT

Each of the undersigned specifically represents to Lender and to Lender's actual or potential agents, brokers, processors, attorneys, insurers, servicers, successors and assigns and agrees and acknowledges that: (1) the information provided in this application is true and correct as of the date set forth opposite my signature and that any intentional or negligent misrepresentation of this information contained in this application may result in civil liability, including monetary damages, to any person who may suffer any loss due to reliance upon any misrepresentation that I have made on this application, and/or in criminal penalties including, but not limited to, fine or imprisonment or both under the provisions of Title 18, United States Code, Sec. 1001, et seq.; (2) the loan requested pursuant to this application (the "Loan") will be secured by a mortgage or deed of trust on the property described herein; (3) the property will not be used for any illegal or prohibited purpose or use; (4) all statements made in this application are made for the purpose of obtaining a residential mortgage loan; (5) the property will be occupied as indicated herein; (6) any owner or servicer of the Loan may verify or reverify any information contained in the application from any source named in this application, and Lender, its successors or assigns may retain the original and/or an electronic record of this application, even if the Loan is not approved; (7) the Lender and its agents, brokers, insurers, servicers, successors and assigns may continuously rely on the information contained in the application, and I am obligated to amend and/or supplement the information provided in this application if any of the material facts that I have represented herein should change prior to closing of the Loan; (8) in the event that my payments on the Loan become delinquent, the owner or servicer of the Loan may, in addition to any other rights and remedies that it may have relating to such delinquency, report my name and account information to one or more consumer credit reporting agencies; (9) ownership of the Loan and/or administration of the Loan account may be transferred with such notice as may be required by law; (10) neither Lender nor its agents, brokers, insurers, servicers, successors or assigns has made any representation or warranty, express or implied, to me regarding the property or the condition or value of the property; and (11) my transmission of this application as an "electronic record" containing my "electronic signature," as those terms are defined in applicable federal and/or state laws (excluding audio and video recordings), or my facsimile transmission of this application containing a facsimile of my signature, shall be as effective, enforceable and valid as if a paper version of this application were delivered containing my original written signature.

Borrower's Signature	Date	Co-Borrower's Signature	Date
X		**X**	

X. INFORMATION FOR GOVERNMENT MONITORING PURPOSES

The following information is requested by the Federal Government for certain types of loans related to a dwelling in order to monitor the lender's compliance with equal credit opportunity, fair housing and home mortgage disclosure laws. You are not required to furnish this information, but are encouraged to do so. The law provides that a lender may discriminate neither on the basis of this information, nor on whether you choose to furnish it. If you furnish the information, please provide both ethnicity and race. For race, you may check more than one designation. If you do not furnish ethnicity, race, or sex, under Federal regulations, this lender is required to note the information on the basis of visual observation and surname. If you do not wish to furnish the information, please check the box below. (Lender must review the above material to assure that the disclosures satisfy all requirements to which the lender is subject under applicable state law for the particular type of loan applied for.)

BORROWER	❑ I do not wish to furnish this information.		CO-BORROWER	❑ I do not wish to furnish this information.	
Ethnicity:	❑ Hispanic or Latino	❑ Not Hispanic or Latino	Ethnicity:	❑ Hispanic or Latino	❑ Not Hispanic or Latino
Race:	❑ American Indian or Alaska Native	❑ Asian ❑ Black or African American	Race:	❑ American Indian or Alaska Native	❑ Asian ❑ Black or African American
	❑ Native Hawaiian or Other Pacific Islander	❑ White		❑ Native Hawaiian or Other Pacific Islander	❑ White
Sex:	❑ Female	❑ Male	Sex:	❑ Female	❑ Male

To be Completed by Interviewer This application was taken by:	Interviewer's Name (print or type)	Name and Address of Interviewer's Employer
❑ Face-to-face interview		
❑ Mail	Interviewer's Signature Date	
❑ Telephone		
❑ Internet	Interviewer's Phone Number (incl. area code)	

Continuation Sheet/Residential Loan Application

Use this continuation sheet if you need more space to complete the Residential Loan Application. Mark **B** for Borrower or **C** for Co-Borrower.	Borrower:	Agency Case Number:
	Co-Borrower:	Lender Case Number:

I/We fully understand that it is a Federal crime punishable by fine or imprisonment, or both, to knowingly make any false statements concerning any of the above facts as applicable under the provisions of Title 18, United States Code, Section 1001, et seq.

Borrower's Signature	Date	Co-Borrower's Signature	Date
X		X	

Sample Truth in Lending Disclosure Statement

TRUTH IN LENDING DISCLOSURE STATEMENT

Creditor	Applicant(s)
Mailing Address	Property Address
Loan Number	Preparation Date

ANNUAL PERCENTAGE RATE	FINANCE CHARGE	Amount Financed	Total of Payments
The cost of your credit as a yearly rate.	The dollar amount the credit will cost you.	The amount of credit provided to you or on your behalf.	The amount you will have paid after you have made all payments as scheduled.
E %	E$	E$	E$

PAYMENT SCHEDULE:

NUMBER OF PAYMENTS	* AMOUNT OF PAYMENTS	MONTHLY PAYMENTS ARE DUE BEGINNING	NUMBER OF PAYMENTS	* AMOUNT OF PAYMENTS	MONTHLY PAYMENTS ARE DUE BEGINNING

* Includes mortgage insurance premiums, excludes taxes, hazard insurance or flood insurance.

DEMAND FEATURE: ☐ This loan does not have a Demand Feature. ☐ This loan has a Demand Feature.

ITEMIZATION: You have a right at this time to an ITEMIZATION OF AMOUNT FINANCED.
I/We ☐ do ☐ do not want an itemization.

REQUIRED DEPOSIT:
☐ The annual percentage rate does not take into account your required deposit.

VARIABLE RATE FEATURE:
☐ This Loan has a Variable Rate Feature. Variable Rate Disclosures have been provided to you earlier.

SECURITY: You are giving a security interest in:

ASSUMPTION: Someone buying this property
☐ cannot assume the remaining balance due under original mortgage terms.
☐ may assume, subject to lender's conditions, the remaining balance due under original mortgage terms.

FILING / RECORDING FEES: $

PROPERTY INSURANCE:
☐ Property / hazard insurance is a required condition of this loan. Borrower may purchase this insurance from any insurance company acceptable to the lender.
Hazard insurance ☐ is ☐ is not available through the lender at an estimated cost of   for a   month term.

LATE CHARGES: If your payment is more than   days late, you will be charged a late charge of   % of the overdue payment.

PREPAYMENT: If you prepay this loan in full or in part, you
☐ may ☐ will not have to pay a penalty.
☐ may ☐ will not be entitled to a refund of part of the finance charge.

See your contract documents for any additional information regarding non-payment, default, required repayment in full before scheduled date, and payment refunds and penalties.
E means estimate.

I/We hereby acknowledge reading and receiving a complete copy of this disclosure. I/We understand there is no commitment for the creditor to make this loan and there is no obligation for me/us to accept this loan upon delivery or signing of this disclosure.

_____	Date	_____	Date
_____	Date	_____	Date

GENESIS 2000, INC. * V9.3/W11.0 * (818) 223-3260   Form RegZD (03/95)

Sample Good Faith Estimate

GOOD FAITH ESTIMATE

Lender:	Sales Price:
Address:	Base Loan Amount:
	Total Loan Amount:
Applicant(s):	Interest Rate:
	Type of Loan:
Property Address:	Preparation Date:
	Loan Number:

The information provided below reflects estimates of the charges which you are likely to incur at the settlement of your loan. The fees listed are estimates - actual charges may be more or less. Your transaction may not involve a fee for every item listed. The numbers listed beside the estimates generally correspond to the numbered lines contained in the HUD-1 or HUD-1A settlement statement which you will be receiving at settlement. The HUD-1 or HUD-1A settlement statement will show you the actual cost for items paid at settlement.

800	ITEMS PAYABLE IN CONNECTION WITH LOAN:		1100	TITLE CHARGES:	
801	Origination Fee @ % + $	$	1101	Closing or Escrow Fee	$
802	Discount Fee @ % + $	$	1102	Abstract or Title Search	$
803	Appraisal Fee	$	1103	Title Examination	$
804	Credit Report	$	1105	Document Preparation Fee	$
805	Lender's Inspection Fee	$	1106	Notary Fee	$
806	Mortgage Insurance Application Fee	$	1107	Attorney's Fee	$
807	Assumption Fee	$	1108	Title Insurance	$
808	Mortgage Broker Fee	$			$
810	Tax Related Service Fee	$			$
811	Application Fee	$			$
812	Commitment Fee	$			$
813	Lender's Rate Lock-In Fee	$			$
814	Processing Fee	$			$
815	Underwriting Fee	$	1200	GOVERNMENT RECORDING AND TRANSFER CHARGES:	
816	Wire Transfer Fee	$	1201	Recording Fee	$
			1202	City/County Tax/Stamps	$
900	ITEMS REQUIRED BY LENDER TO BE PAID IN ADVANCE:		1203	State Tax/Stamps	$
901	Interest for days @ $ /day	$	1204	Intangible Tax	$
902	Mortgage Insurance Premium	$			$
903	Hazard Insurance Premium	$			$
904	County Property Taxes	$			$
905	Flood Insurance	$			$
		$	1300	ADDITIONAL SETTLEMENT CHARGES:	
1000	RESERVES DEPOSITED WITH LENDER:		1301	Survey	$
1001	Hazard Ins. Mo. @$ Per Mo.	$	1302	Pest Inspection	$
1002	Mortgage Ins. Mo. @$ Per Mo.	$			$
1004	Tax & Assmt. Mo. @$ Per Mo.	$			$
1006	Flood Insurance	$			$
				TOTAL ESTIMATED SETTLEMENT CHARGES:	$
"S"/"B" designates those costs to be paid by Seller/Broker.			"A" designates those costs affecting APR.		

TOTAL ESTIMATED MONTHLY PAYMENT:		TOTAL ESTIMATED FUNDS NEEDED TO CLOSE:	
Principal & Interest	$	Down Payment	$
Real Estate Taxes	$	Payoff	
Hazard Insurance	$	Estimated Closing Costs	$
Flood Insurance	$	Estimated Prepaid Items / Reserves	$
Mortgage Insurance	$	Total Paid Items (Subtract)	$
Other	$	Other	$
TOTAL MONTHLY PAYMENT	$	CASH FROM BORROWER	$

THIS SECTION IS COMPLETED ONLY IF A PARTICULAR PROVIDER OF SERVICE IS REQUIRED. Listed below are providers of service which we required you to use. The charges indicated in the Good Faith Estimate above are based upon the corresponding charge of the below designated providers.

ITEM NO.	NAME & ADDRESS OF PROVIDER	TELEPHONE NO.	NATURE OF RELATIONSHIP

These estimates are provided pursuant to the Real Estate Settlement Procedures Act of 1974, as amended (RESPA). Additional information can be found in the HUD Special Information Booklet, which is to be provided to you by your mortgage broker or lender, if your application is to purchase residential property and the Lender will take a first lien on the property.

Applicant	Date	Applicant	Date

Applicant	Date	Applicant	Date

☐ This Good Faith Estimate is being provided by a mortgage broker, and no lender has yet been obtained.

Sample Error and Omissions/Compliance Agreement

LENDER:
BORROWER(S):

PROPERTY ADDRESS:
LOAN NO.:

ERROR AND OMISSIONS/COMPLIANCE AGREEMENT

STATE OF
COUNTY OF

The undersigned borrower(s) for and in consideration of the above-referenced Lender funding the closing of this loan agrees, if requested by Lender or Closing Agent for Lender, to fully cooperate and adjust for clerical errors, any or all loan closing documentation if deemed necessary or desirable in the reasonable discretion of Lender to enable Lender to Mortgage Association, Federal Home Loan Mortgage Corporation, Government National Mortgage Association, Federal Housing Authority or the Department of Veterans Affairs, or any Municipal Bonding Authority.

The undersigned borrower(s) agree(s) to comply with all above-noted requests by the above-referenced Lender within 20 days from date of mailing of said requests. Borrower(s) agree(s) to assume all costs including, by way of illustration and not limitation, actual expenses, legal fees and marketing losses for failing to comply with correction requests in the above-noted time period.

The undersigned borrower(s) do hereby so agree and covenant in order to assure that this loan documentation executed this date will conform and be acceptable in the marketplace in the instance of transfer, sale or conveyance by Lender of its interest in and to said loan documentation, and to assure marketable title in the said borrower(s).

DATED effective _____ this day of _____, 20_____

_____   _____
(Borrower)   (Borrower)
_____   _____
(Borrower)   (Borrower)

Sworn to and subscribed before me_____this day of _____, 20_____

                            _____
                                      (Notary Public)

                            My Commission Expires:

Sample Notice of Right to Cancel

Loan No. _____

NOTICE OF RIGHT TO CANCEL
Your Right to Cancel

You are entering into a transaction that will result in a mortgage on your home. You have a legal right under Federal law to cancel this transaction, without cost, within three business days from whichever of the following events occurs last:
(1) The date of the transaction, which is June 11, 2007; or
(2) The date you received your Truth in Lending disclosures; or
(3) The date you received this notice of your right to cancel.

If you cancel the transaction, the mortgage is also canceled. Within 20 calendar days after we receive your notice, we must take the steps necessary to reflect the fact that the mortgage on your home has been canceled, and we must return to you any money or property you have given to us or to anyone else in connection with this transaction.

You may keep any money or property we have given you until we have done the things mentioned above, but you must then offer to return the money or property. If it is impractical or unfair for you to return the property, you must offer its reasonable value. You may offer to return the property at your home or at the location of the property. The money must be returned to the address below. If we do not take possession of the money or property within 20 calendar days of your offer, you may keep it without further obligations.

How to Cancel

If you decide to cancel this transaction, you may do so by notifying us in writing, at Yourbank, Anywhere, USA.
You may use any written statement that is signed and dated by you and states your intention to cancel, or you may use this notice by dating and signing below. Keep one copy of this Notice because it contains important information about your rights.

If you cancel by mail or telegram, you must send the notice no later than midnight of June 14, 2007 (or midnight of the third business day following the latest of the three events listed above). If you send or deliver your written notice to cancel some other way, it must be delivered to the above address no later than that time.

I WISH TO CANCEL

_____   _____
Customer's Signature   Date

Chapter 10

Credit Cards and Other Open-End Consumer Credit Loans

An *open-end* credit plan is when the creditor reasonably expects repeated transactions, prescribes the terms of the transactions, and provides for a finance charge that may be computed from time to time on the outstanding unpaid balance. A credit card account and a credit line are examples of open-end credit plans. A credit card is, in reality, a loan from a lending institution that pays the merchant within a few days of receiving the loan document (credit card receipt) from the merchant. The lending institution (credit card issuer) then sends you an invoice.

Becoming eligible for a credit card depends upon having a solid credit history — or at least it should. These days, a lot of companies are fairly free and easy about giving consumers cards. More than ever, consumers need to rely on their own financial common sense to sift out the genuine good deals, and not to overindulge and sink into deep credit card debt.

Information That Must Be Disclosed

Before opening any account under an open-end consumer credit plan, the creditor must disclose to you each of the following items, to the extent they apply to your situation:

- the conditions under which a finance charge may be imposed, including the time period (if any) within which any credit extended may be repaid without incurring a finance charge (except that the creditor may, at his election and without disclosure, impose no finance charge if payment is received after the termination of the time period). If no time period is provided for repayment, the creditor must disclose this fact;

- the method of determining the balance upon which a finance charge will be imposed;
- the method of determining the amount of the finance charge, including any minimum or fixed amount imposed as a finance charge;
- where one or more periodic rates (different rates in different time periods) may be used to compute the finance charge, each rate, the range of balances to which it applies, and the corresponding nominal annual percentage rate determined by multiplying the periodic rate by the number of periods in a year;
- identification of other charges that may be imposed as part of the plan, and their method of computation;
- in cases where the credit is or will be secured, a statement that a security interest has been or will be taken in (a) the property purchased as part of the credit transaction, or (b) property not purchased as part of the credit transaction identified by item or type.

> **Example:** Before opening an account under an open-end credit plan, the seller only said that it might, at its option, retain a security interest in merchandise at the time the purchaser bought merchandise. The seller failed to specifically disclose the conditions under which it would retain or acquire any security interest. The failure to disclose was a violation of this section. (Under federal law, a creditor is not allowed to take the following items as collateral unless the loan is being made for the purchase of the items: clothing, furniture, appliances, linens, china, kitchenware, television, wedding rings, and other personal effects.); and,

- a statement of the protection provided as to the creditor's and your responsibilities. With respect to one billing cycle per calendar year, at intervals between six months and eighteen months, the creditor must send a statement to each borrower to whom the creditor is required to send a statement that contains the information as described in the next section.

Since the purpose of this law is to permit informed credit shopping, the required disclosures should be made *before* a credit transaction is completed.

Billing Disclosure Requirements

After the credit is extended, your creditor will send you statements. In each billing cycle, your creditor is required to send you certain information, including:

- the outstanding balance in the account at the beginning of the statement period;
- the amount, date, and a brief description of each extension of credit during the billing period;
- the total amount credited to the account during the period;
- the amount of any finance charge added to the bill during the period;
- if more than one rate is used (for example, a cash advance often accrues a different interest rate from credit card purchases), the breakdown of the charges;
- the total finance charge billed as an annual percentage rate;
- the balance on which the finance charge was computed and a statement of how the balance was determined;
- the outstanding balance in the account at the end of the period;
- the date payment must be made by in order to avoid additional finance charges; and,
- the address to which you are making inquiries about your billing.

Penalties for Violations

The penalties for violating any of the above requirements are the same as those for failure to comply with disclosure requirements for credit as listed in Chapter 9:

- any actual damage sustained by the borrower as a result of the failure;
- twice the amount of any finance charge in connection with the transaction between $100 and $1,000; and,
- the reasonable attorney's fees and costs incurred in a successful legal action.

Consumer Loan Billing Procedures

Billing for consumer loan payments is regulated by the Fair Credit Billing Act (FCBA) (Public Law 93-495). If a bill is incorrect, you should notify the creditor, in writing by certified mail, return receipt requested, within sixty days after the creditor sent you the bill. The notice to the creditor should state your name and account number, that you believe the bill to be incorrect, and your reasons why. (See page 105 for a sample letter.) Unless the creditor then hears from you, the creditor has thirty days after receiving your letter of dispute to send you written acknowledgment of your dispute. Within two billing cycles after that (no more than ninety days), the creditor must make appropriate corrections on your bill, notify you of the corrections, or must make an investigation.

If the creditor's investigation shows that the amount is correct, then the creditor must send you a written explanation, along with any supporting documents. If you have disputed the bill based upon the fact that you have been charged for goods that were never delivered to you, then the creditor should delete the charge, unless it is determined that the goods were actually delivered, mailed, or otherwise sent to you. The creditor must have a statement showing that fact.

A creditor who does not follow the rules under this law forfeits any right to collect from you the amount you have disputed and any finance charge on that amount (total not to exceed $50).

After the creditor has received notice from you under the FCBA, the creditor may not threaten to report adversely to anyone about your credit standing because of your failure to pay the disputed amount, nor may any legal action be taken to collect the amount. You cannot be denied credit because you have disputed a bill.

Unsolicited Credit Cards

The law provides that "no credit card shall be issued except in response to a request or application therefor." (This does not apply to renewal of, or substitution for, a credit card that you previously accepted.) If you receive a credit card without applying for it, the issuing company is fully responsible for its use. However, if you sign the card, use it, or notify the company that you will keep it, then in many states you have accepted the card and will be liable for charges.

Lost or Stolen Credit Card

As the holder of a credit card, you will be liable for the unauthorized use of that card only if:

- the card is an accepted credit card;
- the liability is less than $50;
- the card issuer gives adequate notice to you of your potential liability;
- the card issuer has given you a description of how to notify the card issuer of a loss or theft (this can be printed on the billing statement);
- the unauthorized use is before the card issuer has been notified that an unauthorized use has occurred or may occur as a result of loss or theft; and,
- the card issuer has provided a method whereby you can be identified as the person authorized to use the card.

In order to hold you liable, the card issuer must prove that the use was authorized, or that there are valid reasons for holding you liable.

NOTE: *If you allow someone else to use your card, even if you limit the amount charged and the limit is exceeded, this is not considered unauthorized use.*

New Credit Card Fraud

Credit card fraud appears to be rampant. Be sure to *always* sign the back of your credit card. Be very careful about giving out your credit card expiration date and number, because once this information becomes available to others, almost anything can be purchased with your card and new accounts can be opened in your name.

The Internet is now a location for credit card fraud. Although efforts are being made by credit card companies to combat fraud, such as scrambling card numbers, you should be extremely cautious in using credit cards on the Internet (or anywhere). You might not be aware that your credit card information has been used by someone else until you receive an invoice. Check your statements very carefully. Report the unauthorized use to your card provider immediately.

For Further Research

The laws regarding open-end consumer credit plans are found in United States Code, Title 15, Chapter 41, Subchapter I, Sections 1637 through 1666(j); correction of billing errors is explained in Section 1666. Sample forms as prescribed by the Federal Trade Commission are found in United States Code Annotated, Title 15, and in the Code of Federal Regulations, Title 12, Appendix G.

You should also contact the Federal Trade Commission at 877-FTC-HELP or their website at **www.ftc.gov.**

Sample Letter
Notifying of Incorrect Billing

August 23, 2007

VISA
213 Interest Street
Sometown, Anystate 12045

RE: Account No. 5555-5555-5555
Jane Doe

Dear Sir or Madam:

This letter is to notify you of an error in my July 2007 statement. The amount shown on the statement as being charged for prescriptions from Jake's Pharmacy is $114.00. The total cost of the prescriptions was actually $14.00.

According to the Credit Billing Act, you have 30 days to confirm that you have received this letter unless you correct the item before that time. You then have two billing cycles in which to investigate and either confirm the $114.00 amount or correct the billing.

Enclosed is a copy of my bill from Jake's Pharmacy. Thank you.

Sincerely,
Jane Doe
CERTIFIED MAIL
RETURN RECEIPT REQUESTED
P-396-388-492

Chapter 11

Consumer Lease Disclosures

The types of disclosures that must be made in consumer leases are regulated by the following:

- Truth in Lending Act (TLA) that includes "Truth in Leasing" provisions;
- Regulation M, adopted by the Federal Reserve Board, that contains federal disclosure requirements pertaining to consumer leases;
- the Consumer Leasing Act of 1976 (Public Law 94-240) (the current rules because effective January 1, 1998); and,
- states also have laws regulating leasing, some specifically addressing automobile leasing.

Consumer Lease

A *consumer lease*, as defined in the Act, is a contract for the use of personal property for more than four months, and for a total payment of no more than $25,000, primarily for personal, family, or household purposes. Most commonly leased items are automobiles and furniture. However, any property that is not real estate is included in the regulations. The *lessee* is the person who is offered a lease; the *lessor* is the person offering to lease or arranging to lease under a consumer lease. It makes no difference that the lessee has the option to purchase the property at the end of the lease term.

Disclosure Requirements

You may find an advertisement in the newspaper similar to the following: "Drive a fully equipped automobile for $199 per month.*" The asterisk refers to lease disclosures in small print at the bottom of the ad that you probably will not notice. The ad gets your attention, you visit the dealership, and the salesperson misleads you into thinking you are buying the car rather than leasing it. Worse yet, because it is such a good deal, you decide to trade in your fully paid-for car, but the dealer does not give you credit for its full value.

Before the lease transaction is completed, the lessor should provide you with certain information, set out clearly and accurately. This information includes:

- a brief description of the leased property;
- the amount of any payment required at the time the lease term begins;
- the amount payable by you for any fees, registration, certificate of title, or license fees or taxes;
- the amount of other charges payable by you, which are not included in the periodic payments;
- a description of the charges and that you will be liable for the difference, if any, between the anticipated *fair market value* of the leased property and its appraised actual value at the termination of the lease, if the lease includes such liability;
- a statement of the amount or method of determining the amount of any liabilities the lease imposes upon you at the end of the term, and whether or not you have the option to purchase the leased property and at what price and time;
- a statement setting forth all express warranties and guarantees made by the manufacturer or lessor with respect to the leased property; and identifying the party responsible for maintaining or servicing the leased property together with a description of the responsibility;
- a description of the insurance paid for by you, or the insurance required of you, including the types and amounts of coverage and costs;

- a description of any security interest held or to be retained by the lessor in connection with the lease and a clear identification of the property to which the security interest relates;
- the number, amount, and due date or periods of payments under the lease and the total amount of such *periodic* payments;
- if the lease provides that you will be responsible for paying the anticipated fair market value of the property on expiration of the lease, the lessor must disclose the fair market value of the property at the beginning of the lease, the total cost of the lease at the time it terminates, and the difference between the two amounts; and,
- a statement of the terms under which you can terminate the lease before the end of the lease term and the method of determining any penalty or other charge for delinquency, *default*, late payments, or early termination.

The disclosures can be made in the lease contract to be signed by you. Where the lessor may be unable to provide exact dollar amounts, estimates can be given.

An advertisement by a radio broadcast to aid, promote, or assist in consumer leasing must meet the above disclosure advertisements, state the number, amounts, due dates or periods of scheduled payments and the total payments, and provide a toll-free number for consumers to use. The telephone number must be available for at least ten days from the date of the broadcast.

Residual Value Calculation

The *residual value* is the agreed-upon amount that will represent the value of the property at the end of the lease. If your lease includes an estimated residual value of the property, the estimate must be a reasonable approximation of the anticipated actual *fair market value* of the property at the expiration of the lease. (The fair market value is what a willing buyer would expect to pay.) The estimated residual value may be considered unreasonable if it exceeds the actual value by more than three times a single monthly lease payment. (This does not take into consideration a situation where the property is damaged beyond reasonable wear and tear—the lessor may set standards for reasonable wear and tear.)

If the estimated residual value is greater than three times the actual value, this may also be considered as evidence that the lessor acted in bad faith, and in that case, the lessor cannot collect the excess amount unless a court grants a judgment in favor of the lessor. Of course, you can make a final adjustment with the lessor regarding the excess residual after the termination of the lease.

If a lease has a residual value provision at the termination of the lease, you may, at your own expense, get a professional appraisal of the property by an independent third party agreeable to both the lessor and to you. The appraisal will then be binding on both parties.

Liabilities for Violations

If a lessor has violated any of the requirements under the Consumer Leasing Act, the lessor may be subject to the following liabilities as under other disclosure requirements:

- any actual damage sustained by you as a result of the violation;
- injunctions by federal district courts;
- fines of up to $11,000 per day per violation; and,
- your reasonable attorney's fees and costs incurred if your legal action is successful.

In a successful court action by a lessee, the lessor is required to pay the lessee's attorney's fees. For violations under the Consumer Leasing Act, a court action must be brought within one year of the termination of the lease agreement.

Any penalties or other charges provided for in the lease against the lessee must be reasonable in light of the actual harm caused to the lessor.

For Further Research

The federal laws regarding consumer leases are found in United States Code, Title 15, Subchapter I, Part E, Sections 1667 through 1667(e). The regulations are found in Code of Federal Regulations, Title 12, Part 226, Truth in Lending, Section 226.15.

United States Code, Title 15, Section 1667 (c) addresses the liability of advertisers of consumer leases.

Detailed requirements are also found at **www.ftc.gov/bcp/conline/ pubs/buspubs/adlease.htm**.

Chapter 12

Real Estate Loans

Loans for which we use our real property as security come in many forms. The most familiar is the conventional bank mortgage, in which a bank provides money to purchase a home. However, there are also other types as described below. For most people, this is the largest sum of money they will ever owe, and it is important to understand the differences among the various types of obligations and how the lender can try to recover its money if the debt is not repaid as agreed.

Mortgages

A *mortgage* is a lien the bank or other lender has against your real property, or an interest your lender has in your real property, as security for the note you have signed to pay for the property. (*Real property* refers to real estate; *personal property* usually refers to any other type of property.) Your mortgage is probably your largest debt, and you may need to make formal arrangements to delay payment. The most common form is the institutional mortgage (including *Veterans Administration* (VA) and *Federal Housing Administration* (FHA) mortgages given by banks and savings and loans).

If you have taken out an *equity line* against your home or other real estate, you probably have a second or third mortgage against the property. (The *equity line* is a line of credit given by a lender using the equity you have in your real property as collateral.) If the seller loaned you money to buy the property, he or she probably has a *purchase money mortgage*.

A *second mortgage* is a loan for which some additional value in the real property was given as collateral after the original, or primary, mortgage. In order to help you buy the property, the seller may have given you a second or even a third mortgage. In many cases these are interest only, or amortized over a long period of time with a balloon payment due in five years or so. Also, if a lender loans you money to make improvements to the property (or for other purposes previously explained in Chapter 9), the lender may have taken out a second or third mortgage on your property.

Any other lender who holds a mortgage on your property, or anyone who has a lien against your property either by virtue of a judgment or otherwise (as explained in Chapter 16) besides the first mortgage holder, can foreclose its mortgage. However, when title to the property is transferred at the foreclosure sale, the buyer will get the property subject to the first or prior mortgages.

NOTE: *A mortgage can be foreclosed only through court action.*

The important point to remember is this—if you have several mortgages against your property, keeping the first one current is not enough. If you do not keep the others current, a *foreclosure* action may still be filed by the other mortgage holders, who would then foreclose their interest in your property subject to the first or prior mortgages. They may then pay off the first or prior mortgages.

> **Example:** Bank A has a mortgage on your property. Bank B has a second mortgage. You pay Bank A the regular payments, but not Bank B. Bank B may still foreclose, but takes title to the property subject to the Bank A mortgage.

Contract or Agreement for Deed

In some states, the *Contract for Deed, Agreement for Deed,* or *Land Contract* is still used when title to the property does not actually transfer to the buyer until a certain specified amount of money is paid toward the purchase. Although your seller may have led you to believe that if you do not pay, he may immediately reclaim the property and require you to leave, confirm that fact with an attorney.

In many states, the seller must go through formal foreclosure proceedings just as if title had transferred when the sale was made. The law often provides a purchaser under a Contract or Agreement for Deed with *equitable title* to the property, and will protect that interest as it does the interest of an actual legal title holder. To protect your interest as purchaser of the property, you should determine whether the Contract or Agreement for Deed can be recorded in your local public records. This will put others on notice of your interest in the property.

A seller under a Contract for Deed may require you to sign a *quitclaim deed* at the time you signed the Contract for Deed, allowing the seller to record the transfer of title back to him or her if you fail to make the payments as required. You should check the law in your state to determine whether this is legal. In some states, such a deed or transfer of title back to the seller at the time you signed the Contract or Agreement for Deed would be *void* (or *voidable*).

Deed of Trust

Many states use the *deed of trust* as the form of indebtedness to the lender. This involves three parties — the beneficiary or lender, the trustor or borrower, and the trustee, an independent third party that holds the trust deed. The trust deed is the document signed over by you, the borrower, to the trustee, that gives the trustee the power to sell your property if you fail to make the payments required on the note you signed promising to make payments to the lender.

Your Loan Documents

Your note and mortgage, trust deed, or other loan documents should spell out the terms of your loan, including the total amount of the mortgage and the monthly payments. You may also have a *grace period* — a specified number of days to make the payment — before late payment charges or additional interest can be added. Review all the documents carefully and, if you do not understand them, call your lender and ask. Most mortgages must meet the Truth in Lending requirements explained in Chapter 9.

The Mortgage Foreclosure Process

Although the procedural details may vary from state to state, a mortgage foreclosure generally works like this: Usually after ninety days, your lender will notify you that your payment is late, and that it must be brought current. If that particular payment and subsequent payments are not made, the lender will notify you that if you do not pay the required amount, the lender will begin foreclosure proceedings. (The lender usually uses an attorney at this point.)

A lawsuit is then filed, advising the court that no payments have been received for the specified time period, that the lender is exercising its right to *accelerate* the mortgage, and that the lender is entitled to foreclose its mortgage. In other words, the lender is asking that the property be taken from you by court order and sold to the highest bidder, and that any interest you have be *foreclosed*.

After the lawsuit is filed, you will be either served with a summons, or notice of the foreclosure will be published in the local paper that publishes legal notices. There is a period of time in which responses must be filed. If you do not file any written defenses with the court, which happens often, the case is set for hearing. The judge will then order that the mortgage be foreclosed and that a date for sale be set. Notice of the sale is published, and the property is sold to the highest bidder. (Usually either the sheriff's office or clerk of the court conducts the sale.)

Service of Process and Deficiency Judgments

If the lender or mortgage holder (plaintiff) makes a diligent effort and is still unable to find you in order to have you personally served with the summons from the court, in most cases, notice of the foreclosure lawsuit can be published in a local newspaper. If you are served only by publication—in other words, you are not personally served with a summons, then the lender can take the property and no more. However, if you are *properly* served with a summons, and the property does not sell at the foreclosure sale for the amount awarded in the court's judgment of foreclosure, you may be held personally liable for any deficiency. A *deficiency* is the difference between the amount of the judgment and the lesser amount of the actual sale price. For example, if the judgment was for $100,000 and the property sold for only $90,000, there is a $10,000 deficiency. Again, this will depend upon the terms of your particular note and mortgage.

A deficiency judgment is like any other judgment and the same options are available to the creditor (the former mortgage holder) for collection. In some states, the deficiency judgment is entered automatically; in others, the creditor must go to the court after the sale and ask that judgment be entered.

NOTE: *California does not allow a first mortgage holder to get a deficiency judgment; a few other states restrict the availability of a deficiency judgment.*

You can argue to the court that the lender should not be granted a deficiency judgment against you if the sale price for the property at the foreclosure sale was unreasonably low. The court has the right to look into the relationship between the lender and the buyer of your property and decide whether there was any misconduct or *collusion* (secret agreement between the lender and the buyer), in which case a judge can refuse to enter a deficiency judgment. If the value of the property exceeds the debt, the judge can refuse to give the lender a deficiency judgment against you.

At this stage of the proceeding, you need to present as much evidence as possible to the court, including an appraisal of the property's fair market value, which might cause a judge to decide in your favor. If you can afford it, you may want to have an appraisal of the property done on the date of sale.

If the property sells at the foreclosure sale for an amount higher than the amount of the judgment, plus any added-on legal interest, then you may be entitled to the excess amount.

After the Sale—Period of Redemption

Most states have a *period of redemption* after the sale takes place, where the owner can pay the amount of the judgment to the court, plus any legal interest, and redeem his property. This time period is set by law and varies from state to state. As another possible solution to the foreclosure, you may be able to transfer (or *assign*) this right to redeem your property to someone else, who can then in turn either lease or sell the property back to you.

Foreclosing a Deed of Trust

A trust deed is advantageous to the lender because the lender does not have to go to court to foreclose its loan. If you do not meet your obligations under the note, a notice of default can be recorded in your local county records. *Once it is recorded and you have received a copy, the foreclosure process has begun.* Most states give you a certain period of time, after the notice is recorded and you have received your copy, to reinstate your loan. In order to reinstate the loan, you must bring the payments current and pay any interest and penalties.

After the period allowed for reinstatement has run, the trustee must advertise the property for sale for a minimum period of time. You will find the advertisement in a paper containing legal notices—probably not in your regular newspaper. After the time for advertising has run, the property is sold to the highest bidder. Often the lender (in this case the *beneficiary*) is the highest bidder. Following the sale, your state may give you an additional period of time to redeem the property.

Selling the Property before Foreclosure

If you sell the property before the lender forecloses, your buyer, the title insurance company, or attorney handling the closing will research the title and find that the property has a mortgage or deed of trust (or mortgages or liens) against it. Sometimes a buyer takes title to the property in spite of the mortgage (instead of paying off the mortgage and getting a mortgage release or satisfaction), and assumes and agrees with you that he or she will make the mortgage payments to you or directly to the lender.

However, your obligation to make the payments has not automatically been eliminated.

Many mortgages and notes contain a *due on sale clause*. In other words, if there is a transfer of title without the lender's approval, the lender may declare the entire balance of the mortgage due and payable in full. Although beyond the scope of this book, you should carefully review your loan documents before considering such a transfer. Even if there is no due-on-sale clause, you will not be relieved of the debt. Many bank loans require that a new buyer qualify and pay a certain amount to the bank before the bank will relieve you and accept the new owner as the borrower.

If you do not get a release from your lender, the lender can proceed with foreclosure if your buyer does not make the payments as he promised you. Not only will your buyer be named as a defendant in the foreclosure lawsuit, but you will also be named as a defendant as the person obligated on note and mortgage. The lender may still get a deficiency judgment against you.

> **Example:** Beverly bought a home in Florida from John. John gave Beverly a deed to the property, and Beverly in turn gave John a note and mortgage. John financed 80% of the purchase price of the property. Beverly then sold the property to Charles, and Charles agreed to make the payments to John. When Charles failed to continue making payments, John filed a lawsuit to foreclose his mortgage on the property. Beverly, although she had sold the property to Charles, was named as a defendant in the lawsuit. John had no agreement with Charles—only with Beverly. The property was purchased at the foreclosure sale for less than the amount of money owed on the mortgage plus attorney's fees and court costs. John asked the court to enter a deficiency judgment against Beverly for the difference.

Deed in Lieu of Foreclosure

If you find yourself in a position in which you are simply unable to continue making your payments and cannot sell your property, you may want to suggest to your lender that it take a *deed in lieu of foreclosure*. This is a deed transferring title of the property to the lender, in exchange for the lender's agreement to forego the foreclosure proceeding and forego obtaining a deficiency judgment against you (in a state that allows deficiency judgments in mortgage foreclosures). In your negotiations, you should also ask that the lender allow you to live in the property for a certain period of time after the transfer of title.

Not all lenders will accept this as an alternative, especially if you have other assets and the lender believes it can collect a deficiency judgment. Most lenders would prefer not to own real estate, particularly where the value of the property is less than the amount of the mortgage. However, this is an alternative that you may wish to consider.

A deed in lieu of foreclosure may be a good alternative if the mortgage holder is the person from whom you bought the property. The seller would then have the property back to sell again, and he will also have had the benefit of the down payment you paid when you bought the property.

NOTE: *Since this is recorded in your local public records, a credit reporting agency may report the deed in lieu of foreclosure on your credit report.*

Negotiating with Your Lender

Your lender may also be willing to work with you during *economic hardships* and take partial payments for a period of time, or forego payments until you are able to resume the regular payment schedule. (Particularly in bad economic times, lenders usually do not want to own your real estate—they want the money. Even if they get the property back through foreclosure, they probably will not be able to get the money.) You and the lender are, in most cases, looking for the same thing—a way in which the bank can minimize its losses and you can keep the property. As a result of the large number of delinquencies in home loans, some lenders have even established departments for the specific purpose of working out loan payment problems with borrowers.

When you realize you are having financial difficulties, do the following.

- Set an appointment with the bank's loan department manager, or have a personal meeting with the officer who is in charge of your loan. (You should begin with a positive attitude — that you are willing to work out your financial problem *with* the lender.)
- Explain your circumstances, and that you are committed to meeting your obligations.
- Empathize with the lender's position in a tough financial market.
- If the officer is not responding favorably to your appeal, you should point out that you may consider bankruptcy as an option. This would tie up the property for a considerable length of time, and cost the lender both interest and legal fees. (If you file bankruptcy, the lender probably will not be able to get a deficiency judgment against you.) The officer may well decide it is much better to negotiate with you than to take such a loss.

An individual or private lender may be willing to work with you through your difficult times, particularly if you had previously been prompt in making your payments. In negotiating with a private lender, you should find out what the lender does or intends to do with the loan payment. Perhaps he will extend your loan in exchange for an increase in the interest rate. It is important to consider a number of different alternatives.

FHA Extensions

If you have a Federal Housing Administration (FHA) loan on your house, you may be able to work out an extension of your payments. The FHA insures the loans that institutional lenders make to you. If you default on your FHA loan, the lender may turn the property over to FHA and collect its money. In order to help you stay out of foreclosure, the FHA has a plan that may help you.

If you are behind three months or more on your payments, your lender will send you a letter regarding your default and a form for you to complete explaining your financial situation. After receiving your completed form, the lender can then transfer your loan to the Department of

Housing and Urban Development (HUD). Or, you may contact your local HUD office directly and explain that you have an FHA insured mortgage and that you are unable to make the payments due to circumstances beyond your control (usually an illness or job layoff).

NOTE: *The property must be your primary residence and your only FHA property.*

You must also be able to show that you will be able to begin making payments again within a certain time period. If you meet the requirements, a plan will be worked out and you will have a certain time period to bring the payments current.

More detailed information on this program is available through your local HUD office.

If you have a *balloon payment* (the term usually refers to a payment that is more than twice larger than any other payment under the loan) coming due that you are unable to make, try to get your lender to refinance the loan. You may be able to make larger payments over a period of time and pay off the balance due. With some creative thought and a clear idea of what your lender's objectives are, you may be able to come up with some alternatives to pay the balance due.

All possibilities should be explored before you allow the foreclosure process to go forward, find yourself served with a summons, and then possibly have a deficiency judgment entered against you.

NOTE: *Both the foreclosure action and the judgment will be shown on your credit report and may negatively affect your ability to get credit in the future.*

If You Are in the Military

The *Servicemembers' Civil Relief Act* (revised December 19, 2003) provides an umbrella of protection from civil legal actions for certain military personnel. (U.S.C., Title 50, "War and National Defense Act.") A lender cannot foreclose out of court (on a deed of trust) if you are in the military service. The plaintiff in a court foreclosure action must file a sworn statement with the court stating whether or not you are in the military service. If the plaintiff states that either (1) he does not know or (2) you are in the military service, the court cannot enter a judgment against you until an attorney has been appointed to represent you and the attorney is heard on your behalf. Other protections are now also provided by the new Act.

Recap—Steps You Can Take after Foreclosure Is Started

Recently, the news media has presented numerous stories about foreclosures, particularly in those areas of the country hardest hit economically. Your best approach is to negotiate with your lender *before* the foreclosure process is started and reach an agreement to extend, refinance, or otherwise work out your problem. In some cases, of course, there is not much you can do to prevent the inevitable. Once the foreclosure process has begun, you can still stop or at least delay the process by:

- reaching an agreement with the lender that will reduce your payment for a period of time (*forbearance agreement*). The lender may accept whatever you are able to pay, and accrue the balance owed over time to be added onto the mortgage, or give you an extension, turning the missed payments into a debt payable during or after the original term of the loan;
- if there is a second (or third, etc.) loan against your property, negotiating with that lender to pay off the first loan and incorporate the amount into the second, resulting in only one loan for you to pay;
- reading your loan papers carefully to determine whether you have the right to bring the payments current after foreclosure is filed. (Remember that if the loan is in the form of a trust deed, you should be able to bring the payments current before the notice of sale is published.) If so, you may be able to raise the funds to reinstate the loan — i.e., arrange a loan from a friend, refinance through the same or another lender, take in a co-owner or partner who perhaps will help you bring the loan current in exchange for a portion of the equity in the property, etc. You may even have a family member who is willing to cosign or give you a loan to help you through your crisis;

- in a mortgage foreclosure, filing your written response to the foreclosure action with the court. The court will then allow both you and the lender to present your cases. In your written response, you should dispute any inaccuracies in your lender's figures, inaccuracies in the legal description, or other lender errors, and present as a *counterclaim* against the foreclosure complaint any claim you have against the lender for violation of the Truth in Lending disclosure requirements (see Chapter 9);
- in a mortgage foreclosure action, telling the court that service was improper. Even after the sale, in some instances you may be able to have the entire foreclosure set aside (made null and void) by the court if you can show that you were available to be served by the lender. Yet, instead of personally serving you with a summons, notice was published in the newspaper;
- challenging the trust deed documents in court. By proving to the court that the documents do not include information required by law, the entire foreclosure process can be made null and void. Regulation Z requirements must be met in most situations;
- getting your lender to agree to accept a deed in lieu of foreclosure, if you have no defense and you can avoid a deficiency judgment; or,
- using the threat of (or filing) bankruptcy.

You may have a lawsuit against the lender if they have threatened you or attempted to intimidate you. You should set these facts out in your written defense to the foreclosure. The Federal Trade Commission has the authority to protect you from a lender's unfair and deceptive practices used in foreclosure.

On pages 126–127 is a mortgage Foreclosure Complaint and a sample response (Answer). In your response to a court action, you should first answer each statement made by the lender in the complaint. Then, if you agree that some of the statements made by the lender in the complaint are correct, but you have further explanations or reasons that you believe the court should be made aware of, these should be set out in your answer as *affirmative defenses*. If you have any claim against the lender—for example, violation of a disclosure requirement under Regulation Z, this should be stated in a counterclaim or countersuit along with your answer to the lender's charges.

It is possible to have a foreclosure judgment set aside (withdrawn) even after the redemption period has passed, if you can show to the court that the lender did not make a sufficient effort to find and notify you, or that some other error occurred in the foreclosure action.

Finally, borrowers are fighting back against lenders who were once aggressively competing for the borrowers' business. Lawsuits range from a 1.5 billion dollar claim based on fraud and conspiracy in forcing a silver and oil business into bankruptcy, to damages caused by a lender's delays in processing loans. If you think you may have the basis for a lawsuit against your lender, you should get the advice of an attorney.

For Further Research

To determine whether your state uses deeds of trust or mortgages, simply look at your loan documents. Then obtain information from your lender regarding Regulation Z and contact your regional Federal Trade Commission office for further literature. (see Appendix B.) If your mortgage might be foreclosed, read your state's statutes regarding the legal procedure for filing a foreclosure action, noting the maximum time periods allowed for the various steps in the process.

Note how long you have to redeem your property after the sale. When you research your state's statutes, ask the librarian for an annotated version. This will include cases that might help clarify certain provisions of the law. The cases will also give you an idea of what kinds of defenses other people in situations similar to yours have presented to the court.

Your local law library might have how-to books on mortgage foreclosure defenses, such as those published by your state bar association continuing legal education committee. HUD publishes information about how to avoid foreclosure, available via the website at **www.hud.gov/foreclosure.**

Sample Mortgage
Foreclosure Complaint

IN THE CIRCUIT COURT OF THE NINTH JUDICIAL CIRCUIT IN
AND FOR LEE COUNTY, FLORIDA

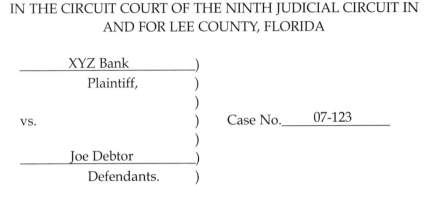

XYZ Bank	)	
Plaintiff,	)	
	)	
vs.	)	Case No. 07-123
	)	
Joe Debtor	)	
Defendants.	)	

FORECLOSURE COMPLAINT

The plaintiff, XYZ Bank, hereby files this complaint as follows:

1. This is an action to foreclose a mortgage on real property located in Lee County, Florida, and for damages in excess of $5,000.00.

2. On or about June 9, 2006, the defendants executed and delivered a note to the plaintiff secured by a mortgage on the real property that is the subject of this action. Copies of the note and mortgage are attached hereto as Exhibits "A" and "B," respectively, and the terms thereof are incorporated herein by reference. The real property that is the subject of this action is described in the mortgage.

3. The defendants failed to pay the installment under the note due, despite demand therefor by the plaintiff.

4. There is now due and owing under the note the principal sum of $39,278.24, together with accrued interest to March 1, 2007 in the amount of $262.50, plus per diem thereafter at the rate of $8.63.

5. The lien represented by the mortgage is superior to the estate or interest of the defendants and anyone claiming by, through, or under the defendants.

6. That the property which is the subject of this action is residential rental property, and that a receiver should be appointed by the court to insure the continued maintenance and care of the subject property.

7. The plaintiff has retained the services of the undersigned law firm and has agreed to pay said firm a reasonable fee for the prosecution of this action.

8. All conditions precedent to the institution of this action have occurred, been performed, or excused.

WHEREFORE, plaintiff prays that judgment be entered in its favor, and for all other relief the Court deems proper.

XYZ Bank by John President   *8-3-07*
Signed   Date

Responding to a Foreclosure Complaint

A complaint for foreclosure will usually contain numbered paragraphs, stating why the mortgage is entitled to foreclose. You will need to respond to each statement in the complaint by either admitting or denying them. The sample answer on pages 128–129 is based on this sample complaint.

NOTE: *Some states require that you explain very specifically in your complaint or answer the facts surrounding your claim; others allow you to be more general and leave the specifics to be spelled out a later date during the court proceedings.*

Sample Answer to Foreclosure Complaint

IN THE CIRCUIT COURT OF THE NINTH JUDICIAL CIRCUIT
IN AND FOR LEE COUNTY, FLORIDA

_____XYZ Bank_____) Plaintiff,)) vs.)) ___Joe and Jane Debtor___) Defendants.)	Case No.___07-123_____

ANSWER

COME NOW the Defendants, _____Joe and Jane Debtor_____
_____, and for their answer to Plaintiff's
Complaint, state as follows:

1. Paragraphs 1 and 2 are admitted.

2. Paragraphs 3 and 4 are denied.

3. Defendants are without knowledge to either admit or deny paragraph 5.

4. Paragraph 6 is denied.

5. Defendants are without knowledge to either admit or deny paragraph 7.

6. Paragraph 8 is denied.

WHEREFORE, defendants respectfully request that the court grant judgment in their favor, and for such other and further relief as the court deems proper.

AFFIRMATIVE DEFENSES

11. The amount currently due under the Note and Mortgage is $72,695.98, not the amount the plaintiff claims is due.

12. Defendants offered plaintiff the amount due on July 23, 2007, but plaintiff refused to accept payment.

WHEREFORE, defendants respectfully request that judgment be granted in their favor, and for such other relief as the Court deems proper.

COUNTERCLAIM

1. Plaintiff failed to provide defendants with the correct financial disclosures as required under the Federal Truth in Lending Act, specifically set forth as follows: Plaintiff failed to properly calculate and inform Defendants of the annual percentage rate of interest.

2. As a result of such failure to provide defendants with the correct financial disclosures, defendants have suffered damages in the amount of approximately $10,000 as follows: Excess interest paid in the amount of $7,248.73, plus additional damages to be proven at trial.

3. Plaintiff has threatened defendants for nonpayment by threatening to contact defendants' employers and neighbors.

WHEREFORE, defendants pray that judgment be granted in their favor in the amount of $10,000, and for such other relief as the Court deems proper.

Dated: September 12, 2007.

Joe Debtor

Jane Debtor

John Debtor & Jane Debtor, Defendants
12 Easy St., Ft. Myers, FL 99999
Tel. (813) 555-5555

Other sample affirmative defenses that may be inserted in the Answer (paragraph 12):

- Defendant was not properly served with summons.
- The property described in plaintiff's complaint is not the property which is described in plaintiff's loan documents.
- Defendant has been properly maintaining the property.

A copy of this answer should be sent to the plaintiff and anyone else required by the court.

Chapter 13

Assessing Your Financial Situation

It is important to periodically assess your financial situation to determine if you are on the right track—reducing your debt and increasing your savings. Regular updates will also alert you to any problems, such as a lender not crediting your account with a payment.

To determine if you have a problem with overwhelming debt, you should ask yourself the following questions—if your answer is "yes" to any of them, then you may be headed for trouble.

- Do you make only minimum payments or skip payments?
- Do you use credit cards for routine household purchases such as groceries?
- Do you have too little or no savings?
- Do you use credit cards to make monthly payments on other credit purchases?
- Do you get calls from creditors or collection agencies demanding payment?

To help you better assess your financial situation, complete the chart on page 134. (If you decide to use credit counseling services, you may be required to complete a similar form.)

First, you should determine exactly what your income and assets are, versus your expenses (referred to as "liabilities"). You may find that you have sufficient income to pay your monthly debt obligations and satisfy your creditors, perhaps at a reduced amount, for a period of time until you are again able to fully meet your obligations. (See the monthly expenses chart on page 135.)

If your income is simply not sufficient to cover your expenses, then you might consider checking for governmental and private sources for which you may be eligible. Government assistance includes unemployment compensation, Aid to Families with Dependent Children (AFDC), food stamps, low-income energy assistance, Medicaid, and Social Security including disability. Churches and community organizations may also provide financial assistance.

You should also eliminate any spending that is not absolutely necessary, such as eating out at restaurants, purchasing that expensive morning cup of coffee, and entertainment. Consider carpooling, or at least combining errands so that the number of trips is reduced. Clip coupons and purchase generic products when available. Most important of all, do not incur new debt.

Second, you should determine which of your assets have been given as security for a debt, such as your car, furniture, appliances, and of course, your home. These will be the assets subject to foreclosure or repossession by the creditor. (See the assets chart at the top of page 136.)

Third, determine which of your assets are currently subject to attachment or levy (i.e., repossession) by a creditor. Perhaps you might consider selling some of these assets to pay down your debt, rather than having a creditor take them to satisfy a judgement. (See the collateral chart on page 136.)

In calculating the extent to which your property is exempt from creditors, be sure to determine whether the property is owned by you and your spouse jointly, and whether you live in a state where the joint property cannot be taken for the debt of only one spouse. (See the assets chart on page 136.)

The liens on your property include any loan made to you for which the property was taken as collateral (i.e., a mortgage or car loan), liens that attach to your property by law (such as contractor's liens), or liens that have resulted from judgments entered against you by a court.

The equity is the amount of money that would be left over when the property is sold and the loans against it (secured creditor) are paid. The equity, if not exempt from creditors, is the amount that would then be available to pay your other creditors.

Your financial health will be determined by comparing your monthly income with your monthly expenses, and by evaluating the amount of equity you have (if any) in your property. The exempt amounts are what would be left to you if your creditors obtained judgments and took your property as payment, or if you file for bankruptcy.

Below is an additional worksheet to help you in determining your equity in your property. Be honest with yourself when completing the form. Often, owners inflate the value of their property. Remember, what you paid for the property is not necessarily what it is worth, nor will you necessarily be able to sell it for as much as you paid.

If you have assets that are secured (i.e., a mortgage against your house or a loan against your car), you must remember that the creditor can take the property for payment of the debt. If the property is valuable and little is owed on your loan, you should consider selling it yourself, paying the creditor, and using the balance left to pay off other debts. (See the Assets Given as Collateral chart on page 136.)

If you have little or no equity in the property (the balance due on the loan equals or exceeds the value), consider selling it and asking the creditor to accept the buyer as the new borrower, releasing you from your obligations (unless the buyer can pay cash). Remember, if the creditor takes steps to repossess the property, any costs, including attorney's fees, may be added on the amount you already owe.

Personal Financial Assessment

NET INCOME (AFTER TAXES):

Source	Monthly Amt.	Non-IRS Exempt? (Y or N)	IRS Exempt? (Y or N)	If Exempt How Much?
Wages				
Social Security				
Pension fund				
Alimony/support				
Public assistance				
Disability				
Other (type)				
TOTALS				*

*The total of the exempt amounts is the amount of income you will be able to keep every month, regardless of any judgment collection efforts or garnishments by creditors. If the IRS is among your creditors, make sure you use the third column to determine your exemptions.

Monthly Expenses

	Amount
Mortgage/rent	
Home maintenance	
Homeowners insurance	
Food	
Food away from home	
Gas/electric	
Water	
Trash collection	
Phone	
Car payment(s)	
Gas/oil/maintenance	
Car insurance	
Other transportation	
Life insurance	
Health insurance	
School/books/tuition	
Child care	
Child support/alimony	
Medical expenses	
Clothing	
Subscriptions	
Cable TV	
Dues/church tithes	
Other	
TOTAL:	$

(Your total monthly expenses, deducted from your total net monthly income listed on page 134, should give you an indication of your financial situation. You may be able to reduce or eliminate some of these expenses in order to pay other debts.)

Assets

	Value	Equity	$ Amt. of Liens on Property	Non-IRS Exempt? (Y or N)	IRS Exempt? (Y or N)
Homestead					
Other real estate					
Automobiles					
Household goods (furniture, appliances)					
Trade tools					
Other (examples: stocks, bonds, CDs, savings)					
TOTALS					

Assets Given as Collateral

Name of Asset	Value	Creditor	Balance of Secured Debt	Equity
House/real estate	$		$	$
Other real estate	$		$	$
Automobile	$		$	$
Automobile	$		$	$
Furniture	$		$	$
Stereo/television	$		$	$
Jewelry	$		$	$
Other	$		$	$
Other	$		$	$

Chapter 14

Repossession of Personal Property

When you buy a car and get financing, you normally give the lender or bank a *security interest* (lien) in the vehicle. Your state might not require any additional notice of the security interest in property to which you hold a title, other than the notice that is placed by the lender directly on the title. On other personal property without a title, the bank or financing company may file what is known as a *financing statement*, which serves the same purpose as a mortgage or deed of trust on real estate. The statement is recorded in the appropriate state office (usually the secretary of state or your county).

It is the lender's duty to make sure that its security interest is properly filed. The financing statement must contain the lender's and your signatures, must clearly identify the property, and must be filed in the correct place.

Just as in a sale of real estate, when you sell the property, the lien must be satisfied or the buyer takes the property with lien still against it (meaning the buyer does not get it without a claim, or "lien-free") and you will still be responsible for payment. The lender can, of course, consent to the transfer of the property and release you from your responsibility. (You may also be violating a provision of your loan agreement and subjecting yourself to criminal and civil prosecution by selling the property without paying off the lender.)

Unless you have an agreement with the lender to the contrary, if you do not pay, or if you otherwise do not live up to your agreement with the lender (such as failing to maintain the required insurance or letting the property deteriorate), the lender has the right to repossess the property as long as there is no *breach of the peace* (violation of public peace by riot, disturbance, or otherwise); for example, violation of a curfew or noise ordinance. The lender may then sell it and get a deficiency judgment against you, much like the mortgage foreclosure process.

> **Example:** If you have repeatedly missed car loan payments at the bank, the bank may contract with someone to repossess the car. Your car can be picked up wherever it can be found. It is then sold, and you may be held responsible for the difference between the amount it sold for and the amount left on the loan, plus attorney's fees and court costs (the deficiency).

Whoever repossesses the property must do so without breach of the peace. In other words, if the property (furniture or appliances, for example) is located in your home, you must consent to the creditor's entry and repossession. Damage to the property by the creditor while it is being repossessed may be considered a breach of the peace.

However, if the property is accessible without entering your home or a closed building, then there is no breach of the peace.

> **Example:** If your car is parked in your driveway, the creditor may walk up, get into the car, and drive it off without violating any law (provided he does not damage the vehicle). If there is damage to your property, you may have a legal case against the lender.

Restrictions on Repossession

The laws regarding secured transactions restrict what the lender can do when repossessing collateral.

- A lender may *not* exert undue pressure on you to repossess an item and has no right to use force.

- A lender is liable to you for any damage caused to the property when it is repossessed.
- A lender may repossess the property without court action only if it can be done without breaching the peace.

Sale of Collateral after Repossession

After repossessing the property, the lender may sell it, lease it, or otherwise dispose of it in a commercially reasonable manner. *Commercially reasonable* generally means that the property must be sold in keeping with the prevailing trade and business practices. The property may be sold in its condition at the time of repossession, or after reasonable preparation for sale by the creditor.

The proceeds of the sale are applied first to the cost of repossession and selling the property, including attorney's fees and legal expenses if provided for in your agreement. Second, the proceeds go to satisfy the outstanding debt. Third, the proceeds satisfy any other *junior security interest* in the property if the secured party has given proper notice to your creditor.

Requirements for Sale

In order for a creditor to sell collateral, the following requirements must be met.

- The creditor should give you reasonable notice of a sale unless you have waived notice.
- The creditor can purchase your property at a private sale only if the property is sold in a recognized market with standard price quotations, and if the sale is commercially reasonable. In determining whether a sale is commercially reasonable, the method of sale, time and place of sale, adequacy of advertising, and appropriateness of wholesale versus retail disposition should be considered.
- The creditor must not allow your property to deteriorate after repossession. To do so may be a violation of the creditor's obligations and will adversely affect the creditor's ability to get a deficiency judgment against you.

Depending upon the terms of your security agreement, you may be liable for any *deficiency* — the difference between the amount of the sale applied to satisfy the debt and the total amount due the creditor. Just as in a mortgage foreclosure, you can argue against the deficiency judgment if you are able to show to the court that the lender sold the property for far too little money.

The lender should also notify you of the sale of the property in order to get a deficiency judgment.

> **Example:** If you loan your car to a friend, the car is wrecked, and the lender accepts the insurance proceeds and turns the car over to the insurance company without notifying you, the lender cannot get a deficiency judgment against you for the balance owed.

If you have paid at least 60% of the cash price of the property, after repossession, the creditor must sell the property within ninety days or you may have a lawsuit against the creditor for *conversion* (taking your property and converting it to the creditor's own use), or as set forth in the section *Your Remedies* in this chapter.

Lender's Pattern of Accepting Late Payments

If your lender has consistently accepted late payments from you, you may have a defense. The lender's conduct led you to believe that late payments would be accepted and that you would be allowed to catch up. The lender's conduct indicated that you should have been given notice of a change in the lender's policy.

Your Remedies

You have several remedies if your lender is attempting to take your property for payment of a debt, including defending the lawsuit or paying to take back the property. Following are some of the options available.

Servicemembers' Civil Relief Act

The *Servicemembers' Civil Relief Act of 1940* provides protections from civil lawsuits or actions for certain military personnel. If you entered into the agreement to buy personal property, such as a refrigerator or automobile, before you entered the military, the creditor cannot repossess the property without a court order. Before allowing the property to be repossessed, the court has the option to decide what is in the best interest of both parties. For example, you might be allowed to keep the property in return for smaller payment amounts to creditor.

No Proper Financing Statement

When the lender attempts to take the collateral, you may argue that the financing statement was not properly filed, or that it failed to contain certain vital information, and that therefore the lender does not have valid security interest in the property.

Your Right to Redeem the Property

Any time before the creditor has sold the property, or before your debt has been paid, you may *redeem* (take back) the property by paying to the creditor all obligations that the property secured plus any expenses the creditor incurred in taking it and preparing for its sale, including reasonable attorney fees and costs.

Reimbursement for Loss

You may recover from the creditor any loss the creditors caused by failing to comply with the requirements regarding repossession and sale of the property. If the property is consumer goods, then you have a right to recover at least the amount of the credit service charge, plus 10% of the principal amount of the debt.

> **Example:** If the creditor repossessed your boat and allowed the physical condition and value to drastically decline while keeping it for many months, failed to follow its normal repossession procedures,

continued to hold it even after it filed its lawsuit for foreclosure, then sold the boat at a price less than half of its value when repossessed, you have a claim against the creditor in that the sale was not "commercially reasonable." (*First Florida National Bank at Pensacola v. Martin,* 449 So. 2d 861 (1984).)

Punitive Damages

Finally, you may be entitled to punitive damages if you can show that the creditor grossly disregarded your rights.

Example: Where a seller had repossessed the buyer's car without warning, seller's agent inventoried the personal property in the car and yet returned the personal property to the car contrary to normal creditor procedure, the court agreed that the seller had shown wanton disregard for the buyer's rights to his personal property and gave the buyer an award of punitive damages against the seller in the amount of $1,000. (*Ford Motor Credit Co. v. Waters,* 273 So. 2d 96, (1973).)

If the Lender Already Has the Collateral

Your lender may have a security interest in your property simply by taking possession of it.

Example: If you have given your bank stocks and bonds to hold as collateral for a note you have signed, the bank may have the right to immediately sell the stocks and bonds if you do not make the required payments. The bank will apply the proceeds from the sale to the unpaid debt, plus any costs of the sale. Unless you have made other arrangements with the lender, the balance, if any is left, should be given back to you.

The same requirements for a commercially reasonable sale of repossessed property apply to a sale of property the lender already has in its possession.

Property Exempt from Creditors

As explained in Chapter 17, the Bankruptcy Act prohibits certain property (exempt property) from being taken by the bankruptcy trustee to satisfy your debts. (In a bankruptcy, either your state or the Bankruptcy Act exemptions will apply.) In other words, you will be able to keep the exempt property even though you have filed for and been discharged by the bankruptcy court.

There are also federal and state laws that exempt certain property from judgment creditors. In this case, *exempt property* is property that a creditor will not be able to take to satisfy a judgment even if you do not file for bankruptcy. The federal exemptions that you may claim (except for seaman's clothing), involve strictly monetary benefits. The federal non-bankruptcy exemptions are set forth in Chapter 17 of this book.

The state exemptions may include your homestead (most states allow only a certain portion of the equity to be exempt), a specified portion of your wages, pension and unemployment benefits, public assistance, insurance benefits, tools you must use in your business, and a certain amount of personal property. In some states, if property is owned by you *and* your spouse, and a judgment is entered against only one of you, the jointly owned property may be unavailable to judgment creditors. (A number of states recognize *tenancy by the entire* property owned by husband and wife, which is usually exempt from the creditors of only one spouse.

You should be aware of and understand your state's exemptions to determine exactly what property may be taken from you for the payment of debts. (California has two alternative lists of exemptions.) You will need this information in order to complete the personal financial assessment in the next chapter. Also, property given as collateral for a loan is not exempt to the extent of the loan, even though it might be listed as an exemption in your state.

Information about exemptions available in your state may be obtained at your local library or the state attorney's office. Remember that the homestead exemption protects your equity in the property to the dollar amount specified by law in your particular state — it does not protect you against foreclosure of a mortgage or loan for which the property was given as collateral.

You should also check with your local court clerk or recorder's office whether or not you must record a statement in the public records listing your exempt property and claiming the exemption, and whether your statement must be published. If at all possible, you should be sure that any required filing is done *before* a lawsuit is filed against you or your property is attached.

If you are in doubt as to whether property a creditor is trying to take from you is exempt, go ahead and assert the exemption as a defense. If the creditor contests your claim, the court will decide. It is better to make the attempt and be refused an exemption, than to allow the creditor to take property you should be able to keep.

For Further Research

Your state statutes should include a section on secured transactions, in which you will find the rights and duties of the lender and borrower set forth in detail. In addition, your state's consumer affairs office should have information available regarding your rights. The applicable provision of the Servicemembers' Civil Relief Act is found in the appendix of the United States Code, Title 50, Appendix Section 521.

It is also available at **www.operationhomefront.org/downloads/SCRA. pdf.**

Chapter 15

When the Creditor Files a Lawsuit

If you have not been able to reach an agreement with your creditors as to how and when payment will be made, there is a good possibility that you will be sued. The goal of the creditor is to get you to pay the debt, or to take your property and sell it in order to pay the debt. Unless the lawsuit is dismissed or withdrawn from the court, a judgment will be entered, either for or against you. (You may be able to work out a "deferred" judgment with the creditor, where the lawsuit is dismissed once payments are made. This will be discussed later in more detail.)

Judgment

A *judgment* is a decision made by a court in a lawsuit. It becomes part of the public records that are available to anyone who takes the time to obtain the information, including credit reporting agencies. A money judgment requires you to pay a certain dollar amount.

How a Creditor Gets a Judgment

A money judgment is obtained by first filing a lawsuit in the appropriate court. A *lawsuit* is an action where the *plaintiff*, the person who files the lawsuit, asks the court to make a determination that he or she is entitled to money from you. The *petition* or *complaint* is the document that the plaintiff files with the court, stating what he or she feels he or she is entitled to and why. In legal terminology, the plaintiff is asking the court for *relief.* (Deficiency judgments are discussed in Chapter 16.) The defendant is the person the lawsuit is filed against and who the plaintiff claims owes the money.

The procedures for filing a lawsuit and getting a judgment vary somewhat from one state to another and are governed by your state court's Rules of Civil Procedure. These rules are available in your state's *statute* books, which you should be able to find at your nearest law library, or perhaps your local public library. Your local court clerk may also be able to answer specific questions, such as how a document must be filed or the time deadline for filing.

Your creditor may file a lawsuit against you if you do not pay the monies you owe. Depending upon the dollar amount the creditor is suing for and your state's laws regulating the court system, the creditor may file on his own in *small claims court,* or a court in which an individual can file without an attorney up to a maximum dollar amount. This is usually the least expensive method of filing a lawsuit that can be used by the creditor.

Attorney's Fees

If you have a written contract with your creditor, or if your state laws so provide, the creditor may be entitled to attorney's fees if he wins the lawsuit and the court enters a judgment against you. If this is the case, the creditor will often choose to use an attorney rather than file the lawsuit himself, even if the dollar amount is small.

Most bank loan documents require that you pay the attorney's fees and costs of any action taken against you to collect the money. You should read the documents carefully to determine whether the attorney's fees are chargeable against you even if the lender is unsuccessful.

If your state has a law that allows attorney's fees to be charged to you only if there is no *justiciable issue* (in other words, there is absolutely no question about your liability for the amount due), then you should by all means raise a defense.

Summons

Once the lawsuit is filed, you must be served with a summons issued by the court, along with a copy of the petition or complaint. *If you are not served with summons and a copy of the petition or complaint, a judgment for payment of money usually cannot be entered against you in the court records.* The summons and petition or complaint will in most cases be served by either a sheriff's deputy or by a special process server appointed by the court.

Answer

You will have a certain period of time to answer the lawsuit after you are served, or a date and time to appear in court will be on the summons. If you are unable to determine your deadline from the papers, call the court clerk in the courthouse where the lawsuit was filed — the clerk should be able to tell you when your answer is due.

If you choose to answer the lawsuit yourself, you should make sure that you respond to each one of the charges set forth in the petition or complaint. A sample Complaint and Answer is included on pages 154–155. If you let your deadline go by without responding or appearing as required, a *default judgment* may be entered against you. In other words, the court may grant the creditor's request and enter the judgment requiring you to pay.

Interest

After the judgment is granted by the court, it may continue to accrue interest until the date it is paid. The amount of interest varies from state to state.

Your Defenses to the Petition or Complaint

If you do not care whether a default judgment is entered against you, and you do not have a defense to any of the charges in the creditor's complaint, then you do not need to do anything. Before you decide to do nothing, however, you should consider the defenses you may have to your creditor's demand for payment. Possible defenses are:

- the creditor has already been paid;
- the service for which the creditor is claiming payment was not performed;
- you are not responsible for payment of the debt (i.e., the debt was incurred by a corporation — not you personally, or by your spouse);
- you were not properly served with summons;
- the *statute of limitations* has lapsed — in other words, the time allowed the creditor to file suit against you for collection of the debt has passed (the statutes of limitations in each state are found in Appendix A);
- the creditor's actions in getting your promise to pay were *unconscionable*, or in other words, so outrageous and overbearing that they would shock the average person. You are telling the court that you were so taken advantage of that you had practically no alternative but to agree to the creditor's terms.

    NOTE: *In order for this defense to be effective, you should have notified the creditor immediately after you agreed to pay that you wanted to cancel your agreement and the reasons why. Your defense would be even stronger if you also refused to make any payments to the creditor and, if the creditor provided you with a service such as roof repair, you immediately requested that he discontinue the work;*

- the goods you received were defective and therefore you do not owe the money;
- the creditor has breached its warranty (i.e., has not met the conditions it is required to meet under the warranty(ies) you received with the goods you purchased). In addition to any written warranties you received when you purchased the goods, there may be *implied warranties* (i.e., warranties that the creditor or seller gives you just by

selling you the product). For example, the goods must be fit for the purpose for which they are intended to be used;

- if a creditor is suing you for a deficiency judgment after repossessing and selling collateral, you may defend on the basis that the sale was not in a *commercially reasonable manner*; and,
- specifically for child support, you have lost your job and request a reduction. (See page 153 for a sample motion of this nature.)

If you were not properly served, the case should not proceed in court. Once you become aware that a judgment has been entered against you based on improper service of summons, you should immediately notify the court clerk and ask about the procedure to have the judgment set aside (i.e., withdrawn from the court records). This may require you to appear in court and present your argument to the judge.

After the lawsuit has been properly filed and summons properly served, there are legally prescribed methods by which the attorney or plaintiff may obtain information from you and other persons regarding the claim. Ultimately, if you do not have any legitimate defenses against the lawsuit and you have been unable to settle with your creditor, the court may enter a judgment against you.

After the judgment is granted by the court, there may also be a certain period of time that you have to appeal the judgment or ask the court to rehear your case and modify or set aside the judgment before the judgment creditor can begin efforts to collect on the judgment. If you have defenses that you did not bring up at the trial or before the judgment was entered, now is the time to let the court know. You may also have the right to appeal your case to a higher court.

Moving to Another State

A creditor can take its judgment into the state where you are currently living or where your assets are located. There is a legal procedure in which the original judgment can become a new judgment in another state. (Check to see if your state has adopted the *Uniform Enforcement of Foreign Judgments Act*.) The new state laws regarding collection of the judgment will then apply to the judgment creditor. You should be notified either by service of a summons or by certified mail from the court clerk that the judgment is being filed, and be given an opportunity to contest the judgment before any action is taken to collect it.

Confession of Judgment

A *confession of judgment* provision in a loan document gives the creditor the right to automatically get a judgment against you if you do not pay the balance owed. Such a provision is prohibited by federal law except in a real estate contract. If your loan document contains such a provision, it is not enforceable by the creditor.

Possible Alternatives if the Debt Is Legitimate

There are several options available to you if the money is legitimately owed and you have no defenses to a lawsuit. Among the options are the following.

Reduced Lump-Sum Settlement

If the debt for which the creditor is demanding payment is legitimate and you have determined that you have no defenses, perhaps your creditor would be willing to settle the debt with you before he obtains a judgment. (As will be discussed in following chapters, *executing* on a judgment is often more difficult than getting the judgment.)

It may be more appealing to your creditor to receive a lump-sum reduced amount as payment in full, rather than go to the time and expense of obtaining a judgment and then attempting to collect the amount due under the judgment.

Deferred Judgment

If the creditor has already filed his lawsuit, and if you are unable to pay a lump-sum amount as settlement in exchange for having the lawsuit dismissed, you might suggest to the creditor that he take a *deferred* judgment. If you pay an agreed-upon amount until the balance due is paid in full, the lawsuit should then be dismissed without a judgment ever being entered against you. However, if you fail to make the required payments, the plaintiff creditor need only properly notify the court, and the court may sign the judgment.

Mediation and Arbitration

As an alternative to court, you can suggest to the creditor that you take your dispute to an independent, third party who will hear both sides. This can be either an arbitrator or a mediator. An *arbitrator* will hear both sides and then make a decision for you just like a court would do. A *mediator* will talk to both sides and attempt to help them come to a mutually acceptable agreement. Some states have mediation programs available to parties in dispute.

Going to Court

If your creditor is unwilling to either settle and dismiss the lawsuit or take a deferred judgment, prepare to go to court. If you are not represented by an attorney, you should have your income and assets well documented, as well as your monthly expenses and your repayment plan. (see Chapter 16.)

When the creditor recognizes that you are making the best effort possible to repay the debt, it is likely that settlement will be reached before the case is actually heard by the judge. In most cases, this will be less costly for the creditor than monthly garnishments or other methods of collecting the judgment amount. If the case is heard by a judge, the judge may order that the creditor accept the amount of money you have offered to pay.

Effect of Judgment on Credit Report

As explained in Chapter 3 ("Items Your Report Cannot Contain"), a judgment may remain on your credit record for a period of seven years, unless the law of the state in which the judgment is entered allows a longer time period. State law may also allow the creditor to periodically renew the judgment, so that it remains effective for a much longer period.

With regard to your credit report, you have the options set forth in Chapter 3. Of course, you should offer an explanation about the circumstances surrounding the judgment to any potential lender who will review the report in making its decision whether or not to loan you money.

For Further Research

Read your state's statutes regarding the legal procedure for filing a lawsuit, noting the maximum time periods allowed for the various steps in the process. When you research your state's statutes, ask the librarian for an *annotated* version. This will include cases that might help clarify certain provisions of the law. The cases will also give you an idea of what kinds of defenses other people in situations similar to yours have presented to the court. (Your court clerk may also have information about mediation or arbitration services.)

The prohibition against a *confession of judgment* clause is found in Code of Federal Regulations, Title 16, "Commercial Practices" Chapter 1, Part 444 (the section of the Federal Trade Commission regulations regarding credit practices).

Sample Motion for Modification

IN THE CIRCUIT COURT OF THE ___6th___ JUDICIAL
CIRCUIT IN AND FOR__Pinellas___ COUNTY, FLORIDA

IN RE:)
   MARY SMITH   )   Case No.__07-ABC____
   a minor   )

<u>MOTION FOR MODIFICATION OF CHILD SUPPORT</u>

   JOHN SMITH, father of MARY SMITH, hereby requests that the court reduce the amount of child support required to be paid under Order dated May 6, 2005, for the following reasons:
   1. I was laid off from my job at XYZ Company on March 15, 2007.
   2. Although I have made a diligent effort, I have been unable to find employment at a salary comparable to what I was making at XYZ Company.
   3. I am currently working as a gardener for ABC Landscaping, and my salary is $6.00 per hour, which is approximately one-half of what I was paid while employed with XYZ Company.
   WHEREFORE, I hereby ask the court that my child support obligation be reduced to $30.00 per week.

John Smith
_____
JOHN SMITH

STATE OF FLORIDA)
COUNTY OF HILLSBOROUGH)
   On this __30th__ day of March, 2007, before me, the undersigned, a Notary Public in and for the above county and State, appeared JOHN SMITH, who is personally known to me to be the same person who executed the above Motion, and that he did so as his free act and deed.

C.U. Sign
_____
Notary Public

My Commission Expires:

Sample Complaint

IN THE CIRCUIT COURT OF THE __6th__ JUDICIAL CIRCUIT, IN AND FOR <u>Pinellas</u> COUNTY, FLORIDA

<u>Easy-Air, Inc.,</u>   )
      Plaintiff   )
)
vs.   )   Case No. <u>07-3592</u>
)
<u>Joe Doe</u>   )
      Defendant

COMPLAINT

Plaintiff, Easy-Air, Inc., a Florida corporation, states as follows:

1. Defendant Joe Doe resides at 1412 Heatstroke Lane, Clearwater, Florida 34616.

2. Defendant Joe Doe entered into an agreement with Easy-Air, Inc. on May 2, 2007, whereby Plaintiff agreed to sell to Joe Doe a new air-conditioning system, to install it and provide any necessary service, for a total price of $2,500.

3. Plaintiff Easy-Air, Inc, delivered and installed the air-conditioning system, but Joe Doe has refused to pay.

4. Plaintiff has performed all of its obligations under the agreement with Joe Doe.

5. Joe Doe is obligated to pay Plaintiff Easy-Air, Inc., for the air-conditioning system and installation.

WHEREFORE, Plaintiff demands judgment against the Defendant, and for Plaintiff's costs and attorney fees.

Easy-Air, Inc.
By:<u>   J.M. President   </u>

Sample Answer to Compl

IN THE CIRCUIT COURT OF THE ___6th___ JUDICl.
AND FOR <u>Pinellas</u> COUNTY, FLORID

<u>Easy-Air, Inc.</u>   )
                    Plaintiff,   )
)   Case No. <u>07-3592</u>
vs.   )
<u>Joe Doe</u>   )
                    Defendant.   )

ANSWER

Defendant, <u>Joe Doe</u>, answers Plaintiff's Complaint as follow

1. Defendant admits paragraph 1 of the Complaint.

2. Defendant admits that he entered into a business transactio with Plaintiff on May 2, 2007, but denies that he agreed to pay Plaintiff.

3. Defendant admits to receiving statements and a demand letter from Plaintiff, and Defendant responded by sending letters to Plaintiff, copies of which are attached to this Answer.

4. Defendant denies paragraphs 4 and 5.

AFFIRMATIVE DEFENSES

1. In exchange for the $2,500.00 Defendant was to pay to Plaintiff, Plaintiff was to deliver to Defendant a new air-conditioning system, fully installed in the Defendant's home.

2. Plaintiff has failed to deliver this item to Defendant; therefore, Defendant does not owe any money to Plaintiff.

WHEREFORE, Defendant demands judgment against Plaintiff.

Joe Doe

Joe Doe, Defendant
1412 Heatstroke Ln.
Clearwater, FL 34616
(813) 555-5555

Chapter 16

Collection of Money Judgments

A creditor who has been successful in obtaining a court order confirming that you do indeed owe a specific amount of money will usually want to proceed to the next step and try to collect, either by taking your property or your income. (Depending upon the amount involved, the creditor may also decide that the cost of attempting to collect the debt is too high to justify the amount that might eventually be recovered. However, the judgement will still remain on your record and be reported on your credit report.) The various ways in which a creditor might attempt to collect are described below.

Actions by a Judgment Creditor

After a creditor gets a judgment against you, he becomes a *judgment creditor*. Once the court enters its judgment, the judgment creditor, if he knows or believes you have or are expecting to receive assets, may attempt to collect the amount due in the judgment in a number of different ways (*execute on the judgment*). The judgment creditor must first determine your assets.

Judgment Creditor's Investigation

If the creditor is unsure of your income and assets, he may obtain this information by taking your *deposition* or asking you to answer *interrogatories* (written questions). Other forms of investigation include checking whether you have a vehicle registered in your name and checking with the property appraiser to find out what, if any, real property you own. If you gave your judgment creditor a financial statement when you obtained the loan, the creditor will also review the statement again to see what assets you represented to him that you own.

In a deposition (or by written interrogatories), the creditor may ask you questions such as the following.

- Are you engaged in your own business and, if so, is the business a sole proprietorship, partnership, or corporation?
- Are you employed? If so, who is your present employer, how much do you earn, and when are your wages paid?
- Do you receive any interest in your employer's business as part of your compensation?
- Do you receive any income from a trust fund?
- Do you receive royalties from any patent, copyright, or invention?
- Do you receive any support from anyone else? If so, from whom and how much?
- Give the names and addresses of all banks in which you have accounts.
- Identify all certificates of deposit, money market accounts, or other accounts where you have money.
- Are you holding any real estate mortgages or other notes (does anyone owe you money)?
- Do you have an interest in a time-share, condominium, or cooperative apartment?
- List your household furnishings, the present value, and whether money is owed against them.
- Do you have any valuable collections (i.e., stamp, coin, antiques, or other)?
- Do you own any jewelry and, if so, what is the value?
- Do you own any automobile(s), boats, airplanes, motor home, etc.?
- Are you a stockholder in a corporation? If so, what is the name of the corporation and the number of shares of stock you own?
- Do you own any bonds or other securities? If so, give a description.

- Do you have an IRA, Keogh, pension, or any other retirement funds?
- Do you have a life insurance policy with a cash surrender value?
- Are you the beneficiary of a life insurance policy?
- Are you the beneficiary under a will of someone who has died, or do you otherwise expect to inherit money or property?
- Is any money held in trust for you?
- Are you expecting a refund on state or federal income taxes paid?

The creditor may also ask to see your latest tax returns and any other records regarding your income and expenses. The purpose is to determine what property you own that the judgment creditor can attach or take to satisfy the judgment. You must respond to the creditor's request or you may be held in contempt of court. Be careful to answer truthfully, as the penalties for perjury may be far greater than the cost of paying your judgment creditor.

When the Creditor Knows What Assets You Have

Once the creditor has obtained information about your assets, he has several options.

> **Example:** A judgment creditor may proceed by garnishing your wages, by seizing an asset such as a car or boat (provided another creditor does not have a prior or *superior claim* to the asset) and selling it, or seizing a bank account.

Some (or all) of your property may be exempt from judgment creditors and the creditor may, by law, be prohibited from taking it. These exemptions are explained in greater detail in Chapter 14. You must be given notice when a judgment creditor is attempting to take your property. The notice should explain how you can file a claim for exemption of the property. The judgment creditor will then either withdraw the attachment or ask for a court hearing.

You are entitled to a hearing to explain to the court that the property is exempt or that it is a basic necessity for you.

Example: If you have a vehicle specially equipped for you due to medical reasons, you will want to explain to the court that the vehicle is absolutely necessary for you to carry out your day-to-day activities, such as grocery shopping.

If you lose the first hearing and your situation changes for the worse, you can ask for a second hearing to explain the change in circumstances to the court and the reasons why the attachment should be withdrawn.

Garnishments

Garnishment is a procedure used by judgment creditors that results in loss of control over your disposable earnings. Under the *Consumer Credit Act,* garnishment is defined as "any legal or equitable procedure through which the earnings of any individual are required to be withheld for payment of any debt." However, a creditor can also garnish other property such as bank accounts. Wage garnishments are the most common.

Wage Garnishments

Congress has enacted laws, contained in the Consumer Credit Act (Sections 1671 through 1677), that restrict the amount of money a creditor can take through garnishment. These laws apply strictly to wages. Congress reasoned that, if garnishment were freely allowed, creditors would unscrupulously encourage the extension of credit, and repayments would take an excessive portion of one's income, creating economic havoc. Garnishments also often result in loss of employment, which has a negative effect on the national economy.

The intent of the law was to grant exemption to wage earners from burdensome garnishments, to protect employment of wage earners, and to prevent bankruptcies. Your state may have its own exemptions. If your state's garnishment laws are even more restrictive, resulting in smaller garnishments, then the state's laws will take priority over the federal laws; if the state's laws are less restrictive, then the federal laws will apply.

After a judgment is rendered against you by a court of law, your creditor may attempt to garnish your wages. The method of garnishment varies somewhat from state to state, but it is generally available to most creditors to collect money owed them. (Some states allow garnishments before a judgment is actually entered by the court; however, the procedure must be strictly followed by the creditor as with prejudgment attachments.)

The Garnishment Procedure—Generally

A notice to withhold a certain amount from your wages is first sent to your employer. In legal terminology, the creditor may now be called the *garnishor*. The employer may now be referred to as the *garnishee*. The garnishee has a certain period of time to respond to the notice ordering the garnishee to pay over to the garnishor certain funds that would otherwise belong to you.

> **Example:** The garnishee may respond by stating that, to the best of his knowledge, you are the head of a household and that therefore your wages are exempt from creditors.

Once the response is received by the garnishor, the garnishor will then decide whether the garnishment should be pursued. This may require a court order. If the garnishment remains intact, then the garnishee must turn the property over to the garnishor. This method of collecting on a judgment is often used as a last resort by creditors, as it is time-consuming and can be expensive.

Federal Exemptions from Wage Garnishment

In some states, the wages of a head of a household cannot be garnished at all; in others, only a small percentage of the net pay can be garnished. Under federal law, which applies if it is more restrictive than your state's garnishment law, the restrictions on garnishment are as follows:

The aggregate disposable earnings (compensation for services) that are subject to garnishment cannot exceed 25% of the wage earner's dispos-

able earnings for that week, or cannot exceed the amount by which the
wage earner's disposable earnings for that week exceed thirty times the
federal minimum hourly wage, whichever is less. If the earnings are paid
other than on a weekly basis, a multiple of the federal minimum hourly
wage equivalent is prescribed by the secretary of labor. (C.F.R., Title 29,
Chapter V, Part 870.10.)

See also **www.dol.gov/dol/allcfr/esa/title_29/part_870/29cfr870.
10htm**.

The restrictions do not apply in the case of a court order for support, a filing under Chapter 13 of the Bankruptcy Law, or any debt due for federal or state taxes. (see Chapter 17.) If you are supporting a spouse or dependent children, the maximum amount of disposable earnings subject to garnishment to enforce a support order (for another spouse or children) is 50%. If you are not then currently supporting a spouse or dependent children, then 60% of the disposable earnings are subject to garnishment to enforce a support order.

If a support garnishment (garnishment of wages to enforce judgment ordering support) has priority and results in the withholding of 25% or more of your disposable earnings, another creditor garnishment may not be permitted.

Depending upon your state's laws, filing of a new garnishment action may be required each time the garnishor wishes to collect money. If so, satisfaction of the creditor's judgment becomes a long and tedious process.

The restrictions apply only to wage garnishments, and not to assignments. If you have assigned a portion of your wages to a creditor, the assignment is not subject to the percentage limitations. If you are potentially subject to having your wages or property garnished, you should make it a point to find out exactly how much of your wages can be garnished and at what time intervals.

Restrictions on Discharge from Employment as a Result of Garnishment

To protect against hardships and disruptions resulting from garnishment of wages, the federal law has also placed restrictions upon employers. Under the federal law, no employer may discharge any employee for the reason that the employee's earnings have been subject to garnishment for any one indebtedness. However, this does not protect you if your wages have been garnished for more than one debt.

If the employer violates the law, he may be subject to a fine of up to $1,000 and imprisonment of up to one year, or both. You may also file a civil action against the employer. Wage garnishments under federal law are regulated by the U.S. Department of Labor.

Non-Wage Garnishments

The judgment creditor may also garnish other money due to you, such as checking account balances and savings accounts. When a bank is served with a garnishment directed at a depositor's account, the bank is not required to determine the depositor's right to a wage earner's exemption under the Consumer Credit Act, the Restriction on Garnishment provisions of the Code of Federal Regulations, or applicable state statutes, and is not required to calculate the amount of the exemption before honoring the garnishment. In other words, the entire account, or the amount required to satisfy the judgment, can be garnished.

Writ of Execution and Levy

The judgment against you may have to be recorded in the public records before the creditor can take any further action.

> **Example:** It may not be sufficient for a creditor to get a judgment against you in order for that judgment to appear as a lien against your real property. The judgment may also have to be filed in the county recorder's office.

NOTE: *If the creditor obtained his judgment in another state or county, there may be certain procedural requirements the creditor must meet in order for the judgment to be valid where the creditor is attempting to collect it.*

If a judgment creditor attempts to attach property, you should determine whether the judgment was properly recorded. If not, you may have a defense to enforcement of the order authorizing the attachment (at least temporarily).

Upon the request of the judgment creditor, the court can enter an order (often included in the final judgment) granting a *writ of execution*. The writ of execution serves as a lien against your property, and is good through the life of the judgment. (Judgments remain as liens on your property for three to twenty years, depending upon the state in which the judgment was entered. Most are valid between ten and twenty years.)

The property subject to the writ of execution may include property acquired *after* the writ of execution has been signed by the court. (In other words, property you get after the judgment is entered may also be taken to pay the judgment amount.) The writ of execution may also contain instructions to the sheriff or other law enforcement officials to levy or take the property identified in the writ of execution. A levy is the absolute legal taking of the property levied on for the payment of a judgment debt. (Although the form used in your particular state may vary somewhat, the intent remains the same.)

The sheriff is required to take as much property as is necessary to satisfy the judgment. Except for real estate, the sheriff must take the property into his possession. If the sheriff breaks into your residence to take the property, he should have a court order to do so. Otherwise, he can only enter your residence peacefully (with your consent).

The property is then sold, and the proceeds are used to pay the judgment. To avoid the levy, the law may allow you to make payment in full on the writ. As mentioned above, you can also appeal to the court explaining, that the property is essential for your livelihood. Once the property is taken, the sheriff is responsible for its loss or destruction.

Forced sale of certain property will be prohibited by law if the property is exempt. (see Chapter 14.)

Attachment of Property Not Yet in Your Possession

The judgment creditor can ask the court for an order allowing him to intercept property that would otherwise come to you, such as a tax refund, commissions, or royalties. You must be given notice of the hearing, and you have the right to explain to the court why the order should not be entered. If it is ordered in spite of your efforts, then a copy is sent to the person holding the property, such as your real estate broker or publisher, and the payments are then made directly to the judgment creditor.

Attachment of Property before Judgment

An *attachment* is a special proceeding authorizing a creditor to take your property *before* he or she gets a judgment. It is granted if the creditor believes you will attempt to delay the court proceedings for collection, that you will move the assets out of reach of the creditor, or that you have an intent to defraud the creditor.

Under normal circumstances, a creditor may not attach your property without first obtaining a judgment and then a writ of execution, as described previously. However, if the creditor has reason to believe that the property will be removed from the court's reach, the court may order the property to be attached.

Example: The sellers of a restaurant sued the buyers for breach of contract, but no final judgment had yet been ordered by the court. The sellers were able to have the buyers' property attached for the reason that the buyers were about to leave the state.

In order to take your property before a judgment is entered:
- the creditor must post a bond;
- the creditor must file an affidavit with the court stating why the property should be attached; and,
- a writ of attachment must be issued by a court of law.

To avoid having your property attached, you also have an opportunity to post a bond that will pay the judgment amount if in fact a judgment is entered. After the property is attached, there must be a hearing at which the grounds for the attachment must be proven by the creditor. If you can prove to the court that you are not intending to move the property from the court's reach, that you are not intending to move from the state, and that you have no intention of defrauding your creditor, then the court should release the writ of attachment.

The legal procedure where property is taken before a judgment is actually entered must be carefully followed by a creditor. As a debtor, you may have a defense that the constitutional requirements of due process were not met before the property was taken. (The due process requirements include the filing of the creditor's affidavit with the court, the filing of a bond by the creditor, the issuance by the court of a writ of attachment, and the opportunity for the debtor to post a bond.)

For Further Research

Read your state's statutes regarding the legal procedure for collection of a judgment, including garnishment, levy, and attachment, noting the maximum time periods allowed for the various steps in the process. When you research your state's statutes, ask the librarian for an *annotated* version. This will include cases that might help clarify certain provisions of the law. The cases will also give you an idea of what kinds of defenses other people in situations similar to yours have presented to the court.

The federal exemptions from garnishment are found in United States Code Annotated, Title 15, Chapter 41, Subchapter II, Restrictions on Garnishment, Sections 1671 through 1677.

PROTECTING YOUR FUTURE CREDIT

Chapter 17

Bankruptcy as an Option

Bankruptcy is a legal and legitimate method of wiping out most, if not all, of your debts. Bankruptcy laws can be traced back hundreds of years. Bankruptcy is usually considered a last resort for credit problems, but if there is no foreseeable change in your income and you are likely to lose everything because of insurmountable debt, then it may be your best alternative.

Contrary to what some of us may believe is a typical bankruptcy filer, most are working persons overwhelmed by credit card debt or hit with an unexpected large expense—usually a huge medical bill or a lost job, for example. According to the Institute for Financial Literacy, a nonprofit organization founded in 2002 to assist people in understanding their finances, an average bankruptcy filer is 25 to 54 years old with a high school diploma or some college education. Many just do not know how to handle money. (For information go to **www.financiallit.org**.)

The bankruptcy laws were enacted to give people overwhelmed with debt an opportunity for a fresh start, and if you are at the point of considering bankruptcy as a real possibility, then you should keep this in mind. It is also important to note that only certain debts, commonly referred to as unsecured debts, can be eliminated by a bankruptcy proceeding. The two most common are debts related to medical treatments and credit cards. Some companies issue "secured credit cards," cards in which the creditor has a security interest in the property you are purchasing using the card.

Other than the exempt property used to pay current debts, the law assumes you have no resources when you file for bankruptcy.

Example: If you own a vehicle worth $8,000, and the exemption allowed by your state is $1,000, then the bankruptcy court will require that the vehicle be sold and used to pay your unsecured debts. In this case, the loss of your property may not be worth using the bankruptcy process to eliminate your debt.

Congress, in the *Bankruptcy Reform Act of 1994*, also made it more difficult for an ex-spouse to use bankruptcy to eliminate debts resulting from a property settlement agreement. However, the exception to discharge only applies if the ex-spouse has the ability to pay and the detriment to the other spouse outweighs the fresh-start benefit of bankruptcy. Alimony and child support are priority debts that must be paid first.

If a credit card was used to pay income taxes, the credit card debt cannot then be eliminated through bankruptcy.

Types of Bankruptcy and Changes to Bankruptcy Procedures

The recent federal *Bankruptcy Prevention and Consumer Protection Act*, signed into law in April 2005, resulted in major reforms to the previous bankruptcy law. There are still three different chapters of the United States Bankruptcy Code under which an individual can file—these are Chapter 7, Chapter 11, and Chapter 13. (A special Chapter 12 bankruptcy, beyond the scope of this book, has been reserved for farmers and family fisherman. Bankruptcy under Chapters 11, 12, and 13 may generally be referred to as a "Reorganization.")

A Chapter 7 case is a liquidation of your debt, a case in which a court-appointed trustee sells your nonexempt assets and distributes the proceeds among your creditors. In Chapter 13, a repayment plan is filed with the court that obligates the debtor to pay some or all of the debts over several years. Under the new bankruptcy law, many consumer debtors will be required to file a Chapter 13 bankruptcy and agree to a five-year repayment schedule. Chapter 11 is primarily used by businesses that need to reorganize in order to get out from under debt. (The major airlines Delta, Northwest, and United, as well as businesses such as K-Mart, are examples of large companies that have filed under Chapter 11.) In Chapter 11, the debtor proposes a plan for paying some or all of the debts, and his creditors get a chance to vote on the plan. (Chapter 11 may be available to consumer debtors in some instances, which are also beyond the scope of this book.)

The new bankruptcy law provides revised guidelines for the dismissal of Chapter 7 (total liquidation) cases or conversions to Chapter 11 or 13 proceedings, which are business and personal plans for debt restructuring and repayment. The law, which took effect October 17, 2005, was designed to make it more difficult for people to erase their debts under Chapter 7 bankruptcy. For the first time, it also requires financial education, making it mandatory that consumers go through financial counseling with an agency approved by the U.S. Trustee's office to consider alternatives before filing for bankruptcy, and to attend a debtor education workshop after bankruptcy.

The decision to consider bankruptcy is often influenced by the actions of creditors in trying to collect a debt. By filing for bankruptcy, your creditors are prevented from doing anything further to harass you during the case. This is referred as the *automatic stay*. Your creditor would not, for example, be able to make phone calls or send letters attempting to collect, or file a lawsuit (or proceed under an existing lawsuit) to collect a debt.

Following is a summary of the two types of bankruptcy available for individuals.

Chapter 7—Debt Liquidation

Counseling is now mandatory prior to filing for bankruptcy, even when it is apparent that a repayment plan is not possible. Participation in a counseling program is required, but accepting the agency's repayment plan is not. However, if the agency does propose a definite repayment plan, it must be submitted to the court, along with a certificate showing that the credit counseling program was completed, before a petition for bankruptcy can be filed. Once the bankruptcy case is completed, attendance at another counseling session is required to learn personal financial management. (Only when proof has been submitted to the court that this requirement has been completed will the court discharge your debts.) A list of approved credit and debt counseling agencies can be found on the U.S. Trustee's website, **www.usdoj.gov/ust.** (Click on "Credit Counseling and Debtor Education.") The credit counseling service is not without cost, and the consumer is usually expected to pay (although some counseling agencies either waive or discount their fees).

In order to determine whether you will be able to file for bankruptcy under Chapter 7 and "discharge" or eliminate all of your debts, you must compare your current monthly income—averaged over the most recent six months before filing for bankruptcy—to the median income in your area for your family's size. The median income can be found in the "Means Testing Information" section of the U.S. Trustee's website. You will be able to file for bankruptcy under Chapter 7 if your income is less than or equal to the median; if your income is greater than the median, you must take an additional step or "means test" to determine if you qualify for Chapter 7 filing. (see "Chapter 13—Repayment Plan" on page 173.) The purpose of this step is to determine if your income, after subtracting certain required debt payments and allowed expenses, is enough to make payments under a Chapter 13 repayment plan. Information about the "means test" can be found on the U.S. Trustee's Web page and the forms can be found at **www.uscourts.gov/rules/new_and_revised_official_forms_101405.htm.**

In a Chapter 7 case, the court will appoint a trustee to represent the interests of your creditors. A month or so after filing, you must attend a so-called "meeting of creditors" with the trustee to answer questions regarding your assets, debts, and so forth. After the meeting, the trustee sells (liquidates) the property that can be taken from you, and distributes the net proceeds among your creditors. After your property has been sold and money distributed to the creditors, the court schedules a final hearing and discharges your debts. The result is that you will no longer legally owe your creditors, and they are forbidden from trying to collect any debts that were discharged in the bankruptcy proceeding.

Trustee

The bankruptcy trustee appointed by the court will hold a meeting of your creditors to allow the creditors to ask questions regarding the debt owed to them. The trustee will also take all of your assets over and above those you are allowed by law to keep (*exempt* assets) and sell them. The proceeds of the sale will be used to pay the trustee for his or her services, any administrative expenses, and ultimately your creditors. (In most cases there is no money left to pay the creditors.) If there are no objections to your bankruptcy filed with the court, an order will then be entered discharging you from all your debts.

If you do not cooperate with the bankruptcy trustee or comply with a court order, or if your debts are consumer debts and you could pay them off with modest effort between three to five years, then your request for a discharge may be denied by the court. However, as a practical matter, most people who file under Chapter 7 are granted a discharge in bankruptcy.

Chapter 13—Repayment Plan

If you did not qualify to file for bankruptcy under Chapter 7, you may file under Chapter 13, which requires repayment of at least some of your debt.

An individual with regular income may file under Chapter 13 if unsecured debts total less than $307,675 and secured debts total less than $922,975. There is no "exempt" property under Chapter 13 as under Chapter 7, since a repayment plan is used to pay off your obligations.

Filing for bankruptcy under Chapter 13 (wage earner) begins with the same forms as under Chapter 7, plus a workable plan for repayment. The repayment plan is prepared by you or your attorney. The district court where you file may have a specific form for a Chapter 13 plan, which must be followed; however, it is usually your responsibility to classify the debts and make a repayment proposal. The bankruptcy court then approves the repayment plan, and you will begin sending payments directly to the Chapter 13 trustee shortly after filing. The trustee is then responsible for payments to creditors according to the terms of the court-approved plan.

After the creditors have been repaid, the court will schedule a hearing, at which time your debts will be discharged.

If your plan would pay all of your outstanding debts, you can complete the plan early. However, if you did not file a plan to pay all of your debt, and your increased income makes it possible to complete the plan early, then the increase must be included in your bankruptcy estate and the U.S. Trustee will most likely require you to amend the plan.

Bankruptcy Exemptions

Under the federal bankruptcy law and state laws, certain property is exempt and cannot be used by the trustee to satisfy your creditors. These exemptions vary from state to state. However, your state exemptions may apply in lieu of the federal bankruptcy exceptions. The following property is exempt (double for married couples) (U.S.C., Title 11, Sec. 522):

- homestead real property, including co-op or mobile home, to $18,450; unused portion of homestead to $9,250 may be applied to any property;
- life insurance payments for person you depend on and need for support;
- life insurance policy with loan value, in accrued dividends or interest to $9,850;
- unmatured life insurance contract, except credit insurance policy;
- alimony, child support needed for support;
- pensions and Retirement Benefits ERISA — qualified benefits needed for support;
- $475 per item in any household goods up to a total of $9,850;
- health aids;
- jewelry to $1,225;
- lost earnings payments;
- motor vehicle to $2,950;
- personal injury compensation payments to $18,450;
- wrongful death payments;
- crime victims' compensation;
- public assistance;

- Social Security;
- unemployment compensation;
- veterans' benefits;
- tools of trade—books and equipment to $1,850; and,
- Wild Card—$925 of any property plus up to $9,250 of any amount of unused homestead exemption.

Additional or different exemptions allowed by individual states may apply if:
- the state you lived in for the 730 days (two years) before filing;
- you did not live in a single state in the previous two years, you use the state where you lived the majority of the 180-day period preceding the two-year period; or,
- the preceding renders you ineligible for any exemptions, then the debtor is allowed to choose the federal exemptions.

Some pension plans and funds in an educational retirement account may also be exempt. In addition, as of April 20, 2005, restrictions on the homestead exemption apply:
- the exemption for a homestead is limited to $125,000 if the property was purchased within the previous 1,215-day (or 3.3 years) period (excepting any interest transferred from your previous principal residence that was acquired before the beginning of the 1,215-day period);
- the value of the state homestead exemption is reduced by any addition to the value brought about on account of a disposition of nonexempt property made by the debtor (made with the intent to hinder, delay, or defraud creditors) during the ten years prior to the bankruptcy filing; and,
- an absolute $125,000 homestead cap applies if either:
    - the court determines that the debtor has been convicted of a felony demonstrating that the filing of the case was an abuse of the provision of the Bankruptcy Code, or

♦ the debtor owes a debt arising from a violation of federal or state securities laws, fiduciary fraud, racketeering, or crimes or intentional torts that caused serious bodily injury or death in the preceding five years.

NOTE: *This limitation is inapplicable if the homestead property is "reasonably necessary for the support of the debtor and any dependent of the debtor."*

Reaffirming a Debt

In a Chapter 7 case, it is still possible to *reaffirm* a particular debt rather than have the creditor take the property and have bankruptcy court discharge the debt to that creditor. A *reaffirmation agreement* would be signed by you and the creditor, stating that you will pay all or a portion of the money owed, despite the bankruptcy filing. In return, the creditor will promise, as long as payments are made, that the property will not be repossessed. If you are not represented by an attorney in your bankruptcy case, any reaffirmation agreement must be approved by the bankruptcy judge. There is a cooling off period in which you will be able to cancel the reaffirmation agreement if you change your mind.

Pros and Cons

Opinions vary as to the effect of a discharge in bankruptcy. Most experts agree that bankruptcy should be used only as a last resort, primarily because of the negative effect it may have on your credit record. The bankruptcy filing will stay in the credit reporting agency's file for a period of ten years. If you are at the point of considering bankruptcy, then your credit report probably is not very high on your list of priorities.

The primary concern of most people who are considering bankruptcy is the inability to get credit after discharge. However, with the large number of bankruptcy filings, some lenders are changing their attitudes. Once all your debts are discharged, you have that much more disposable income to repay a loan. The fact that you have more money available and cannot file Chapter 7 bankruptcy again for another six years may provide the lender a certain level of comfort in giving you a loan.

Finally, many individuals and businesses are now filing for protection from creditors under the bankruptcy laws. Although feelings of guilt and failure are often associated with bankruptcy, remember that the primary purpose of the law is to provide a fresh start.

How to File for Bankruptcy

You can file for bankruptcy with the assistance of an attorney. The attorney's fee must be disclosed in the bankruptcy petition. You can also file for bankruptcy on your own. Before attempting to file your own bankruptcy, you should familiarize yourself with the forms and procedures.

For Further Research

The full text of the bankruptcy laws are found at United States Code, Title 11. The exemptions are found at United States Code, Title 11, Section 522. The Federal Trade Commission currently offers a pamphlet "FTC Facts For Consumers—Before you File for Personal Bankruptcy," available at **www.ftc.gov/bcp/edu/pubs/consumer/credit/cre41.htm**.

Chapter 18

Divorce, Debt, and Community Property

Marriage is typically the joyful and hopeful union of two people, and most often the union of their assets as well as their financial obligations. The smiling couple plans to buy a house, have children, and live happily ever after. Divorce, on the other hand, is often an emotionally and financially devastating experience.

Marriage and Debt

Most couples begin their married lives by opening up joint bank accounts, signing jointly on leases, mortgages, and car loans, and applying for credit in both names. This joint effort may help in obtaining credit that either one of the parties on his or her own would not be able to get. When a joint credit account is opened, the assets, credit history, and income of both parties are combined and considered by a prospective creditor. On the other hand, both parties are then responsible for repayment of any credit extended on a joint application. For credit reporting purposes, the account history must be reported in both names. Each spouse is fully liable.

Of course, each spouse can maintain an individual account as well, which will not be affected by the other spouse's credit. (Except in community property states, as discussed later.) If an individual account holder authorizes another to use the credit (for example, a gasoline credit card given by a parent to a student), the account holder, not the user, is responsible for repayment. For credit reporting purposes, a credit report is issued both in the account holder's and the authorized user's name.

Property Settlements and Court Judgments

If the marriage ends in divorce, division of debt can become at least as important an issue as division of assets. Many times, a divorce settlement or court judgment will set forth which party is responsible for payment of which obligations. The separated or divorced spouses rely on such a document, assuming they are no longer liable for the debt, and are surprised when contacted by a creditor for payment. However, neither a settlement agreement nor a court judgment will relieve a spouse of any debt jointly entered into with the other spouse.

Family Residence

If your former spouse kept the family residence and agreed to make the mortgage payments, you may have given him or her a *quitclaim deed* and assumed that you had no further liability. However, if you have any doubt about his or her financial reliability, you should consider checking periodically to make sure the payments are current. If the lender forecloses, you will be named in the lawsuit as a defendant since you are still obligated on the mortgage.

Credit Rating

To minimize the risk of losing your good credit rating, or finding yourself unable to meet financial obligations because your former spouse may fail to pay the debts that were assumed by him or her in divorce, you might be better off selling as many of your joint assets as possible to pay off the liabilities. In exceptional situations, a creditor might be willing to let you off the hook; for example, if your spouse puts up more collateral for repayment. You might also be able to take a security interest in the property transferred to your former spouse, which will be released when the debts are paid. This would provide you with an asset to sell should the creditor come to you for payment. On real estate, require that your former spouse obtain a new mortgage in his or her own name, and that the mortgage in joint names be paid in full.

Debt Assumed in Divorce

A property settlement agreement with your ex-spouse does not relieve you of any debt you jointly obligated yourselves to pay. If, for example, you and your ex-spouse used a joint credit card, you will both be held liable for payment. A property settlement agreement may specifically spell out which spouse will take over payment of certain bills. However, if your former spouse fails to make the payments as required under your agreement, the creditor will look to you for the money. You can argue that, by agreement, he or she is responsible for the debt. Unless the creditor released you from any obligation to pay, you may still be held responsible. This is also true of your day-to-day service providers.

> **Example:** Bruce had been divorced for over a year and was planning to remarry. Before his remarriage, he received notice that his former wife had filed bankruptcy, thereby eliminating her obligation on the debts she had agreed to pay. The property settlement Bruce had reached with her, which was filed in the court records, described each debt and which party would accept responsibility for payment. However, the creditors had not released Bruce, and when his wife filed for bankruptcy, they looked to Bruce for payment. Bruce was able to manage fine with his portion of the debt as divided in the settlement agreement, but was unable to carry his former spouse's financial obligations as well. Bruce filed for Chapter 7 bankruptcy.

NOTE: *The Bankruptcy Reform Act of 1994 made it more difficult, but not impossible, for an ex-spouse to eliminate debt owed under a property settlement agreement. If you believe your ex-spouse has the ability to pay, you should file an exception to the bankruptcy proceeding. (see Chapter 17.)*

Example: Even if your former spouse has agreed to pay your child's medical bills, you may be held responsible. If you take your child for medical treatment, the physician will most likely look to you for payment. The physician is not a party to any agreement you may have with a former spouse.

If possible, you should make advance arrangements with your former spouse and the service provider for payment of these types of bills, so that ultimately, nonpayment will not have a negative effect on your credit report.

Quitclaim Deed

Finally, if your former spouse kept the family residence and agreed to make the mortgage payments, you may have given him or her a *quitclaim deed* and assumed that you had no further liability. However, if you have any doubt about his or her financial reliability, you should consider checking periodically to make sure the payments are current. If the lender forecloses, then you will be named in the lawsuit as a defendant since you are still obligated on the mortgage.

Community Property and Debt

The states of Alaska, Arizona, California, Idaho, Louisiana, Nevada, New Mexico, Texas, Washington, and Wisconsin have some type of community property legislation. *Community property* describes the unique property interests of husband and wife under these states' laws. For example, income earned by one spouse may be considered community property; that is, property belonging to both husband and wife. Typically, all property of either spouse, regardless of how it is titled (individually or as "husband and wife"), is considered community property unless proven otherwise (separate property must be defined in a contract or proven to be separate), and includes all property acquired during the marriage by either spouse, any income from and increase in value to any such property), and any property purchased from income earned during the marriage. If a business owned by one spouse before marriage increases in value during the marriage, the increase may be considered community property. Both spouses have the full right to manage and control the community property, including any sales, leases, gifts, etc. In some cases a marriage contract can be entered into, which supercedes the community property laws.

In community property states, generally all debts incurred during a marriage, regardless by which spouse, are considered *community debts*. Even if only one spouse signs, these are debts viewed as for the benefit of community of both spouses, or for the benefit of the other spouse. (An exception exists if the spouses have, either by contract or otherwise, defined their separate property; however, the spouse not incurring the debt may still be liable to the extent of any benefit received from the debt.)

> **Example:** If the husband purchases a dishwasher and signs the financing agreement without the cosignature of his wife, his wife may still be held liable because the dishwasher benefitted both spouses.

Separate Property

Even if the spouses have clearly identified separate property, the separate property can be used to satisfy a debt that was otherwise designated a community debt—both husband and wife received a benefit from the debt. Although various aspects of debt incurred during a marriage may be different under community property laws, the same suggestions in dealing with creditors apply as in noncommunity property states.

The Innocent Spouse and the IRS

Most married taxpayers file a joint income tax return; in some cases one spouse will sign, unaware of the details contained in the return or the financial dealings of the other spouse. Even so, the innocent spouse can be held liable for the money due to the Internal Revenue Service, regardless of whether you have been separated or divorced in the meantime. The new tax law, known as *Innocent Spouse Relief* (in addition to *Separation of Liability* and *Equitable Relief*), attempts to assist spouses who, in spite of the fact that they signed the tax return, were totally unaware of any unreported income, incorrect deductions, credits, or other irregularities that resulted in assessment of additional taxes, and who did not knowingly benefit from any such irregularities.

Assistance is also available if you filed a joint tax return, and the IRS took your refund to satisfy your spouse's or former spouse's past due tax, a federal debt such as a student loan or child support. Because community income and expenses are attributed equally to both husband and wife in community property states, a special provision exists for assistance to spouses in those states.

To obtain relief, one of several different forms, depending upon the situation, must be filed with the IRS. Detailed information about the forms and circumstances in which it is appropriate to file are found in IRS Publication 971. Publication 971, and the forms, are available on the IRS website, **www.irs.gov**, or call 800-829-1040.

Chapter 19

Reestablishing Good Credit

Many of the suggestions for first establishing a good credit history described in Chapter 4 apply to reestablishing good credit as well. It becomes necessary to prove to prospective creditors and lenders that you have become a financially responsible person. It may be a painful and slow process, but you must be persistent. On the other hand, people who have completed bankruptcy proceedings and whose debts have been discharged by the U.S. Bankruptcy Court may receive unsolicited offers for new credit cards. The credit card companies apparently recognize that the individual is virtually debt free following the bankruptcy court discharge, and therefore will have more income with which to make future credit card payments. Keeping in mind that one must wait at least seven years before filing for bankruptcy again, it is extremely important to follow the rules for responsible use of credit.

Because of the credit history with less-than-perfect payment record, the costs of credit will most likely be higher than for someone with a good credit report. For example, until interest rates began to rise recently, many homeowners were encouraged to refinance their mortgages. However, someone with a bad credit history would most likely be required to pay a higher rate, and therefore not able to take advantage of the potential savings.

One of the first ways to reestablish good credit is to open a savings account. This not only shows that you are able to control your spending, but the money may also be used as collateral for obtaining a secured credit card. Lenders who extended credit to you in the past—and whom you paid in a timely manner—may be willing to provide credit again. This is particularly true if the reason for your debt problem was not simply over-spending, but an unexpected event such as a major medical expense.

Individual retail establishments may be more willing to extend store credit, such as a gas or store credit card. A gasoline credit card usually requires payment in full each month, and may be easier to obtain than a regular credit card. The manager of your local hardware or tire store may understand the background of your financial problems, and be more will-ing to extend new credit. If a retail store is unwilling to extend credit, try using its purchase layaway plan. If you handle the payments responsibly, it is more likely that the store will then approve your credit application.

However, remember to be selective about applying for credit. Each time a lender checks your credit history, a notation will be made in your credit file. If you have made too many applications, credit may be denied simply because of excessive inquiries.

As already described in Chapter 4 and as mentioned above, another way of reestablishing credit is by using a "secured" credit card. With this method, after you open your savings account, you will be issued a credit card that can be used up to the amount you have in the savings account.

You will pay interest on the amount charged just as with any other card, even though the payment is guaranteed by the collateral in your savings account. To reestablish good credit, you should use the new secured card to create a debt, then pay the amount in full when you receive your invoice. This should be repeated until the lender is con-vinced that you are handling the credit responsibly, and the pattern of paying in full and on time is reflected in your credit report.

Reestablishing good credit is a very individual and personal undertak-ing. How it is accomplished will vary depending upon your current financial situation, the reason for and the extent of the credit problems, your banking relationships, familial relationships (particularly if you need a cosigner), and the likelihood that you will be able to handle future debt obligations.

Chapter 20

Planning the Future

While taking care of your current financial problems, you should also be thinking about the future. A job loss or long-term illness is rarely anticipated, but should be considered when making your decisions about how to handle your income and assets.

Tough economic times catch most people by surprise — they find they have to do whatever is necessary to get by, including getting family members to pitch in with income from part-time jobs. Saving for a rainy day is always recommended by financial planners — some are now even urging people to have a full year's living expenses available in the event of a major setback.

Saving a full year's living expenses is not easy when you are just trying to meet your monthly obligations. Making sure your property is safe or exempt from creditors is a step you can begin taking now. Before doing anything, however, make an honest assessment of where you are financially.

The best way to begin your financial planning is through a realistic budget. Begin by using the Personal Financial Assessment and the Monthly Expenses charts in Chapter 13, then prepare a budget. Since most of our payments are due on a monthly basis, a monthly budget is the easiest for most people to create and use.

There are many computer software programs that are specifically designed to assist in creating a personal budget, or you can make your own by listing in detail all of your income and all of your expenses.

Begin by adding up your salary, wages, and all other forms of income, such as royalties, child support, interest, etc. Next, total up all of your expenses. For expenses paid other than on a monthly basis—such as real estate taxes, which are not included in your mortgage payment—you should determine how the total is broken down by month. If your annual tax bill is $1,200, payable in January, you should include an expense for taxes of $100 per month. This amount should then be set aside to be used exclusively to pay the annual bill. The expense list should be separated into two parts—the first to include all fixed and unchangeable expenses, such as mortgage or rent payment, utilities, food, car payments, and the second to include only *discretionary* expenses—those that you may choose to eliminate, such as restaurants, entertainment, and certain hobbies. Out-of-the-ordinary expenses, such as Christmas and birthday gifts, back-to-school supplies, and summer camp, should also be included. Then compare your total income with your total expenses. There should be enough income left to cover incidentals, such as a home repair expense or auto repair. Finally, as you list your expenses, it is important to remember your financial goals.

If your budget shows that your expenses exceed your income, some changes will be necessary. Check your discretionary expenses to see what can be eliminated. Following are some important tips to help with the budget and planning process:

- be realistic—include only definite income sources (not a "possible" inheritance);
- include all expenses, even those payable quarterly or annually;
- include yourself (savings) as an expense;
- differentiate between fixed expenses and discretionary expenses, and be willing to cut out what you do not really need;
- calculate whether refinancing your mortgage would reduce your debt; and,
- consider selling an asset and using the proceeds to pay off a debt.

Making Yourself Judgment Proof

Finally, you should consider methods by which you can make yourself judgment proof. Being *judgment proof* does not mean that a judgment cannot be entered against you — it simply means that anyone who has a judgment against you will be unable to collect it because any property you do own is exempt. As explained in previous chapters, certain property will be exempt from creditors, including judgment creditors and, in some cases, even the IRS.

If you have assets that you want to keep from potential creditors' hands, you may want to take more drastic measures. For instance, consider moving to a state with exemptions that would allow you to keep those assets.

Example: If you have a large amount of cash, you may want to move to a state with an unlimited homestead exemption and put your cash into your homestead.

Warning: If you are expecting a judgment to be entered against you in the near or immediate future, before transferring property in order to avoid the judgment creditor, contact an attorney. The transfer may be attacked by the creditor as a fraudulent conveyance. The same holds true if you are thinking about filing bankruptcy. A transfer can be set aside by the bankruptcy court as a preference. Proper planning in these instances should include sound legal advice.

Glossary

A

acceleration. To speed up; to bring future obligations current.

adjudication. The act of a court of law making an order or judgment.

affidavit. A sworn, written declaration, usually signed before a notary public.

assignment (of wages or other property). To transfer an interest in certain property to another.

audit. An official examination of accounts and records.

B

beneficiary. Person designated to receive funds or other property from an estate or trust.

bond. A written promise of another (surety) to pay a debt in the event the debtor fails to pay.

C

civil remedies. The legal means of enforcing a civil (as opposed to criminal) right.

collateral. Security (usually property) pledged for the payment of a loan.

collection agency. A business that collects outstanding bills for other businesses and individuals, typically in exchange for a percentage of the amount collected.

complaint. The first document filed in a civil lawsuit.

compliance. Acting in accordance with certain legal requirements.

consolidation. Act of combining two or more debts into one.

consumer. Usually an individual who purchases and/or uses goods and services.

consumer lease. A lease or rental agreement, typically for a vehicle or household goods, between a business and an individual.

contingent liability. A liability that does not become effective until another acts or fails to act in accordance with an agreement.

counterclaim. A claim filed by an individual against whom a first claim has already been filed by another individual or business.

creditor. An individual or business to whom one owes a debt.

credit report. A summary of credit information on an individual that is prepared by a credit reporting agency.

credit reporting agency. A business that assembles and evaluates consumer credit information for the purpose of providing credit reports to third parties.

D

damages. The estimate money equivalent of an injury or wrong.

deadbeat list. List of those who owe money but have failed to pay.

deed of trust. Similar to a mortgage, title to property held by a trustee until a debt affecting real property is paid in full.

default. Failure to meet an obligation, such as a loan payment or court appearance.

deferment. Postponement, particularly of collecting a debt.

deficiency. The amount by which a creditor's claim is not satisfied; and the notice thereof to the debtor.

deposition. Statement taken under oath that is to be used in court proceedings.

disclosure. The act of revealing certain information, particularly to a debtor regarding his loan.

E

economic hardship. Financially severely difficult.

equitable title. The right of ownership, although legal title is held by another.

equity. The amount of value of property remaining after deducting the mortgage and other pledges or liens rightfully against the property.

equity line. A line of credit, or loan, given by a lender with the equity in real estate given as collateral.

execute. To carry out the terms of a legal document, especially a judgment.

F

fair market value. Price at which a willing buyer and willing seller will trade.

file segregation. Establishment of a new credit identity with inaccurate information.

financial statement. A statement, usually requested by a lender, that describes your property, its value, your income and liabilities (debt), indicating your actual financial condition.

forbearance. Refrain from doing something (i.e., collecting a debt).

foreclose/foreclosure. The termination of all of the rights of the borrower in property given as collateral to the mortgagee or lender.

G

good faith. With good intentions (i.e., with most accurate information available).

governmental instrumentality. An agency of the government.

guarantor. One who guarantors the debt or obligation of another.

guaranty. A pledge or promise given as security for payment of a debt or obligation.

I

indemnification. Act of agreeing to compensate someone for any loss or damage.

J

joint and several liability. Referring to financial obligations, all signers are jointly as well as individually liable for the debt.

judgment. A court decision.

judgment proof. Immune from results of a judgment (i.e., having no assets from which a creditor can collect a money judgment).

junior interest. An interest (typically in property) that is inferior to another's interest.

L

lender. A person or entity that loans money to another.

lien. A claim against property for the payment of a debt or obligation.

M

mortgage. The pledge of property as security for a loan, usually real property.

N

negligence. To omit doing something through indifference or carelessness.

O

obligor. One who is obligated to act (i.e., one who owes money).

open-end credit. A sum of money made available to an individual against which amounts can be drawn repeatedly and at various interest rates, such as a credit card or equity-line mortgage.

P

periodic rates. Interest rates that change from time to time as specified in the loan documents.

personal property. Any property that is moveable as opposed to real estate or fixed to real estate. Also referred to as chattel.

petition. *See complaint.*

principal. The amount of money borrowed (as opposed to interest).

pro rata. In proportion to something; according to a certain rate.

public record. Records that are kept by a governmental body and available to the public for review.

punitive damages. Compensation awarded for an injury or wrong that is intended to punish the one who committed such injury or wrong.

purchase money mortgage. Mortgage given by the buyer back to the seller of property.

Q

quitclaim deed. Transfer of title to real estate that does not contain any guaranties or warranties.

R

real property. Real estate; land.

Regulation Z (Reg Z). Federal Truth-in-Lending regulations found in the Code of Federal Regulations, Banks and Banking section.

remedies. The means of enforcing a right.

repossess. To regain possession of something; also used when the creditor is taking possession of collateral after default in the payments by the debtor.

rescission. Withdrawal or cancellation.

residential mortgage transaction. Transaction with the lender whereby real property is given as collateral in exchange for funds.

residual value. The value of property at the end of a specific time period, especially at the end of a lease term.

right of set-off. Typically a lender's right to take money from a borrower's other accounts to pay for a specific debt owed that lender.

S

secured. Protected (pledge of property to assure a creditor of payment).

security interest. An interest in property given as collateral for a debt.

separate property. An individual's property that is not commingled with another's property.

statutes. A written law that is passed by a governing authority, usually a state legislature or Congress.

statute of limitations. A statute stating the period of time in which a claim can be brought before a court.

superior claim. A claim against property, usually by a lender, that takes priority over another claim (i.e., that must be paid before another claim against the same property can be paid).

T

tenants by the entireties. A manner of holding title to property by husband and wife, recognized in nearly one-third of all states, whereby each party holds title to the entire property, and it cannot be divided without the consent of both husband and wife.

U

underwriting. To assume liability for something to the extent of a certain dollar amount.

unsecured. Unprotected; without security.

V

void/voidable. Without legal force or effect/to cause to be without legal force or effect.

W

willfully. Intentionally.

writ. A legal document ordering an authorized person to do a certain act (or to refrain from doing something).

Appendix A

State Resources

Alabama

Consumer Affairs Division
Office of the Attorney General
11 South Union Street
Third Floor
Montgomery, AL 36130
334-242-7335
800-392-5658
www.ago.state.al.us

Alaska

Consumer Protection Unit
Office of the Attorney General
1031 West 4th Avenue
Suite 200
Anchorage, AK 99501
907-269-5100
Fax: 907-276-8554
www.law.state.ak.us

Arizona

Consumer Protection and
Advocacy Section
Office of the Attorney General
1275 West Washington Street
Phoenix, AZ 85007
602-542-3702
800-352-8431
Fax: 602-542-4377
www.azag.gov

Consumer Protection
Office of the Attorney General
400 West Congress
South Building
Suite 315
Tucson, AZ 85701
520-628-6504
800-352-8431
Fax: 520-628-6532
www.azag.gov

Arkansas

State Offices
Consumer Protection Division
Office of the Attorney General
323 Center Street
Suite 200
Little Rock, AR 72201
501-682-2341
800-482-8982
Fax: 501-682-8118
www.ag.state.ar.us

California

State Offices
Bureau of Automotive Repair
California Department of
Consumer Affairs
10240 Systems Parkway
Sacramento, CA 95827
916-255-4300
800-952-5210
916-322-1700 (TDD)
Fax: 916-255-1369
www.autorepair.ca.gov

California Department of
Consumer Affairs
1625 North Market Boulevard
Sacramento, CA 95834
916-445-1254
800-952-5210
www.dca.ca.gov

Office of the Attorney General
Public Inquiry Unit
P.O. Box 944255
Sacramento, CA 94244
916-322-3360
800-952-5225
Fax: 916-323-5341
www.caag.state.ca.us

County Offices
Consumer and Environmental
Protection Unit
Solano County District Attorney's
Office
600 Union Avenue
Fairfield, CA 94533
707-421-6859
707-421-6800
Fax: 707-421-7986

Consumer & Environmental
Protection Division
Fresno County District Attorney's
Office
1250 Van Ness Avenue
2nd Floor
Fresno, CA 93721
559-488-3836
559-488-3156
Fax: 559-495-1315

Contra Costa County District
Attorney's Office
627 Ferry Street
Martinez, CA 94553
925-646-4620
Fax: 925-646-4683

Consumer Fraud Unit
Stanislaus County District
Attorney's Office
P.O. Box 442
Modesto, CA 95353
209-525-5550
Fax: 209-525-5545
www.stanislaus-da.org

Consumer Affairs Division
Napa County District Attorney's
Office
931 Parkway Mall
P.O. Box 720
Napa, CA 94559
707-253-4059
Fax: 707-253-4041

Consumer & Environmental Unit
San Mateo County District
Attorney's Office
400 County Center
3rd Floor
Redwood City, CA 94063
650-363-4651

Consumer Protection Division
Monterey County District
Attorney's Office
P.O. Box 1131
Salinas, CA 93902
831-755-5070
Fax: 831-755-5068

Consumer Protection Unit
Santa Clara County District
Attorney's Office
70 West Hedding Street
West Wing
4th Floor
San Jose, CA 95110
408-792-2880
Fax: 408-279-8742
www.santaclara-da.org

Economic Crime Division
Consumer Fraud Department
County Government Center
1050 Monterey Street
Room 223
San Luis Obispo, CA 93408
805-781-5856
Fax: 805-781-1173
www.sloda.com

Consumer Protection Unit
Marin County District Attorney's
Office
Hall of Justice, Room 130
3501 Civic Center Dive
San Rafael, CA 94903
415-499-6495
Fax: 415-499-3719

Consumer Protection Unit
Santa Barbara County District
Attorney's Office
1112 Santa Barbara Street
Santa Barbara, CA 93101
805-568-2300
Fax: 805-568-2398

Division of Consumer Affairs
Santa Cruz County District
Attorney's Office
701 Ocean Street
Room 200
Santa Cruz, CA 95060
831-454-2050
831-454-2123 (TDD/TTY)
Fax: 831-454-2920
www.co.Santa-Cruz.ca/us

Consumer Mediation Section
Ventura County District Attorney's
Office
800 South Victoria Avenue
Ventura, CA 93009
805-654-3110
Fax: 805-648-9255
www.ventura.org/vcda

Consumer/Environmental
Protection Unit
Orange County District Attorney's
Office
401 Civic Center Drive
West Santana, CA 92701
714-347-8706
Fax: 714-568-1250

City Offices
Kern County District Attorney's
Office
1215 Truxtun Avenue
3rd Floor
Bakersfield, CA 93301
661-868-2340
Fax: 661-868-2700
www.co.kern.ca.us/da/criminal.asp

Santa Monica City Attorney's Office
1685 Main Street, Room 310
Santa Monica, CA 90401
310-458-8336
Fax: 310-395-6727
www.pen.ci.santa-
monica.ca.us/atty/
consumer_protection

Colorado

Consumer Protection Division
Colorado Attorney General's Office
1525 Sherman Street
5th Floor
Denver, CO 80203
303-866-5189
800-222-4444
Fax: 303-866-5691

ElderWatch
A program with the Colorado
Attorney General and the AARP
Foundation
Fighting elder financial abuse and
fraud through information, referrals
and consumer advocacy.
1301 Pennsylvania
#280
Denver, CO 80203
800-222-4444 (option 2)

County Offices
El Paso and Teller Counties District
Attorney's Office
105 East Vermijo
Suite 205
Colorado Springs, CO 80903
719-520-6002
Fax: 719-520-6006
www.dao.elpasoco.com

Weld County District Attorney's
Office
P.O. Box 1167
Greeley, CO 80632
970-356-4010
Fax: 970-352-8023

Pueblo County District Attorney's
Office
201 West 8th Street
Suite 801
Pueblo, CO 81003
719-583-6030
Fax: 719-583-6666

Connecticut
Department of Consumer
Protection
165 Capitol Avenue
Hartford, CT 06106
860-713-6050
Fax: 860-713-7239
www.ct.gov/dcp

Delaware
Fraud and Consumer Protection
Division
Office of the Attorney General
Carvel State Office Building
820 North French Street
Wilmington, DE 19801
302-577-8600
800-220-5424
Fax: 302-577-2496
www.state.de.us/attgen

District of Columbia
Office of the Attorney General for
the District of Columbia
441 4th Street NW
Suite 450 N
Washington, DC 20001
202-442-9828
Fax: 202-727-6546

Office of Consumer Protection
Department of Consumer and
Regulatory Affairs
941 North Capitol Street NE
Washington, DC 20002
202-442-4400
Fax: 202-442-8390
www.dcra.dc.gov

Florida
Florida Department of Agriculture
and Consumer Service
Division of Consumer Services
2005 Apalachee Parkway
Terry Lee Rhodes Building
Tallahassee, FL 32301
850-922-2966
800-435-7352
www.800helpfla.com

Economic Crimes Division
Office of the Attorney General
PL-01 The Capitol
Tallahassee, FL 32399
850-414-3300
866-966-7226
Fax: 850-488-4483
www.myfloridalegal.com

Multi-State Litigation and
Intergovernmental Affairs
Office of the Attorney General
PL-01 The Capitol
Tallahassee, FL 32399
850-414-3300
866-966-7226
Fax: 850-410-1630
www.myfloridalegal.com

Regional Offices
Office of the Attorney General
110 SE 6th Street
Fort Lauderdale, FL 33301
954-712-4600
Fax: 954-712-4658

Economic Crimes Division
Office of the Attorney General
135 West Central Boulevard
Suite 1000
Orlando, FL 32801
407-999-5588
Fax: 407-245-0365
www.myfloridalegal.com

Economic Crimes Division
Office of the Attorney General
Concourse Center 4
3507 East Frontage Road
Suite 325
Tampa, FL 33607
813-287-7950
Fax: 813-281-5515

Economic Crimes Division
Office of the Attorney General
1515 N. Flagler Avenue
Suite 900
West Palm Beach, FL 33401
561-837-5000
Fax: 561-837-5109

County Offices
15251 Roosevelt Boulevard
Suite 209
Clearwater, FL 33760
727-464-6200
727-464-6088 (TDD/TTY)
Fax: 727-464-6129
www.pinellascounty.org

Broward County Consumer
Affairs Division
115 South Andrews Avenue
A460
Fort Lauderdale, FL 33301
954-357-5350
Fax: 954-765-5309
www.broward.org/consumer

Dade County Economic Crime Unit
1350 NW 12th Avenue
Miami, FL 33136
305-547-0671
Fax: 305-547-0717
www.miamisao.com

Pasco County Consumer Affairs
Division
7530 Little Road
Suite 140
New Port Richey, FL 34654
727-847-8106
Fax: 727-847-8191

Hillsborough County Consumer
Protection Agency
8900 N. Armenia Avenue
Suite 226
Tampa, FL 33604-1072
813-903-3430
Fax: 813-903-3432
www.hillsboroughcounty.org/
consumerprotection

Georgia

Governor's Office of Consumer
Affairs
2 Martin Luther King, Jr. Drive SE
Suite 356
Atlanta, GA 30334
404-651-8600
800-869-1123
Fax: 404-651-9018
http://consumer.georgia.gov

Hawaii

Department of Commerce and
Consumer Affairs
345 Kekuanaoa Street
Room 12
Hilo, HI 96720
808-933-0910
Fax: 808-933-8845

Office of Consumer Protection
Department of Commerce and
Consumer Affairs
235 South Beretania Street
Room 801
Honolulu, HI 96813
808-586-2636
Fax: 808-586-2640

Department of Commerce and
Consumer Affairs
1063 Lower Main Street
Suite C-216
Wailuku, HI 96793
808-984-8244
Fax: 808-243-5807
www.hawaii.gov/dcca/ocp

Idaho
Consumer Protection Unit
Idaho Attorney General's Office
650 West State Street
Boise, ID 83720
208-334-2424
800-432-3545
Fax: 208-334-2830
www.state.id.us/ag

Illinois
Consumer Fraud Bureau
1001 East Main Street
Carbondale, IL 62901
618-529-6400
800-243-0607
877-675-9339
Fax: 618-529-6416
www.illinoisattorneygeneral.gov

Consumer Fraud Bureau
100 West Randolph
12th Floor
Chicago, IL 60601
312-814-3000
800-386-5438
Fax: 312-814-2593
www.illinoisattorneygeneral.gov

Governor's Office of Citizens
Assistance
222 South College
Room 106
Springfield, IL 62706
217-782-0244
800-642-3112
Fax: 217-524-4049
www.illinois.gov

Consumer Fraud Bureau
Office of the Attorney General
500 South Second Street
Springfield, IL 62706
217-782-1090
800-243-0618
877-844-5461
Fax: 217-782-1097
www.illinoisattorneygeneral.gov

City Offices
Daley Center
Room 208
50 W. Washington
Chicago, IL 60602
312-744-4006
312-744-9385 (TDD)
Fax: 312-744-9089
www.cityofchicago.org/
ConsumerServices

City of Des Plaines Consumer
Protection Office
1420 Miner Street
Des Plaines, IL 60016
847-391-5006
Fax: 847-391-5378

Indiana
Consumer Protection Division
Office of the Attorney General
Indiana Government Center South
402 West Washington Street
5th Floor
Indianapolis, IN 46204
317-232-6201
Fax: 317-232-7979
www.in.gov/attorneygeneral

County Offices
Marrion County Prosecuting
Attorney's Office
251 East Ohio Street
Suite 160
Indianapolis, IN 46204
317-327-3522
Fax: 317-327-5409
www.indygov.org

Iowa
Consumer Protection Division
Office of the Attorney General
1305 East Walnut Street
2nd Floor
Des Moines, IA 50319
515-281-5926
888-777-4590
Fax: 515-281-6771
www.IowaAttorneyGeneral.org

Kansas
Consumer Protection & Antitrust
Division
Office of the Attorney General
120 SW 10th
2nd Floor
Topeka, KS 66612
785-296-3751
800-432-2310
Fax: 785-291-3699
www.ksag.org

County Offices
Johnson County District Attorney's Office
Johnson County Courthouse
100 North Kansas Avenue
Olathe, KS 66061
913-715-3003
Fax: 913-715-3040

Kentucky

Consumer Protection Division
Office of the Attorney General
The Capitol
Suite 118
700 Capitol Avenue
Frankfort, KY 40601
502-696-5389
888-432-9257
Fax: 502-564-2894
www.ag.ky.gov

Consumer Protection Division
Office of the Attorney General
8911 Shelbyville Road
Louisville, KY 40222
502-429-7134
Fax: 502-429-7129

Louisiana

Consumer Protection Section
Office of the Attorney General
1885 North 3rd Street
Baton Rouge, LA 70802
225-326-6465
800-351-4889
Fax: 225-342-326-6499
www.ag.state.la.us

County Offices
Consumer Protection Section
Jefferson Parish District Attorney
200 Derbigny Street
Gretna, LA 70053
504-368-1020
Fax: 504-361-2899

Maine

Office of Consumer Credit
Regulation
35 State House Station
Augusta, ME 04333
207-624-8527
800-332-8529
Fax: 207-582-7699
www.mainecreditreg.org

Consumer Protection Division
Office of the Attorney General
6 State House Station
Augusta, ME 04333
207-626-8800
www.maine.gov

Maryland

Consumer Protection Division
Office of the Attorney General
200 St. Paul Place
16th Floor
Baltimore, MD 21202
410-528-8662
888-743-0023
Fax: 410-576-7040
www.oag.state.md.us/consumer

Regional Offices
Consumer Protection Division
Maryland Attorney General's
Office
138 East Antietam Street
Suite 210
Hagerstown, MD 21740
301-791-4780
410-576-6372 (TDD/TTY)
Fax: 301-791-7178

Consumer Protection Division
Eastern Shore Branch Office
Office of the Attorney General
201 Baptist Street
Suite 30
Salisbury, MD 21801
410-543-6620
Fax: 410-543-6642
www.oag.state.md.us

County Offices
Howard County Office of
Consumer Affairs
6751 Columbia Gateway Drive
Columbia, MD 21046
410-313-6420
Fax: 410-313-6453

Montgomery County Division of
Consumer Affairs
100 Maryland Avenue
Suite 330
Rockville, MD 20850
240-777-3636
240-777-3679 (TDD)
Fax: 240-777-3768
www.montgomerycountymd.gov/
consumer

Massachusetts

Executive Office of Consumer
Affairs and Business Regulation
10 Park Plaza
Suite 5170
Boston, MA 02116
617-973-8787
888-283-3757
Fax: 617-973-8798
www.mass.gov/Consumer

Consumer Protection and
Antitrust Division
Office of the Attorney General
McCormack Building
One Ashburton Place
Boston, MA 02108
617-727-2200
www.mass.gov/ago

Southern Massachusetts Division
Office of the Attorney General
105 William Street
New Bedford, MA 02740
508-990-9700
Fax: 508-990-8686

Western Massachusetts Division
Office of the Attorney General
1350 Main Street
4th Floor
Springfield, MA 01103
413-784-1240
Fax: 413-784-1244

Central Massachusetts Division
Office of the Attorney General
One Exchange Place
Worcester, MA 01608
508-792-7600
Fax: 508-795-1991

County Offices
Northwestern District Attorney's
Office
13 Conway Street
Greenfield, MA 01301
413-774-5102
Fax: 413-773-3278

Consumer Protection Division
North Western District Attorney's
Office
1 Gleason Plaza
Northampton, MA 01060
413-586-9225
Fax: 413-586-9225

Berkshire County Consumer
Advocates, Inc.
150 North Street
Room 34
Pittsfield, MA 01201
413-443-9128
800-540-9128
Fax: 413-496-9225

Norfolk District Attorney's Office
Consumer Protection Division
1515 Hancock Street
4th Floor
Quincy, MA 02169
617-769-6118
Fax: 617-769-6101

Consumer Council of Worcester
County
484 Main Street
2nd Floor
Worcester, MA 01608
508-754-1176 ext 130
Fax: 508-754-0203

City Offices
City of Boston Consumer Affairs &
Licensing
Boston City Hall
Room 817
Boston, MA 02201
617-635-3834
Fax: 617-635-4174
www.cityofboston.gov/
consumeraffairs

Cambridge Consumers' Council
831 Massachusetts Avenue
Cambridge, MA 02139
617-349-6150
Fax: 617-349-6148
www.ci.cambridge.ma.us/
~Consumer

Greater Fall River/New Bedford
residents contact:
One Government Center
Fall River, MA 02722
508-324-2672
Fax: 508-324-2668

Consumer Protection Program
Haverhill Community Action, Inc.
25 Locust Street
Haverhill, MA 01830
978-373-1971
Fax: 978-373-8966

Cape Cod residents contact:
Consumer Assistance Council, Inc.
149 Main Street
Hyannis, MA 02601
508-771-0700
800-867-0701
Fax: 508-771-3011
www.consumercouncil.com

Consumer Protection Program
Greater Lawrence Community
Action Council, Inc.
305 Essex Street
Lawrence, MA 01840
978-681-4990
Fax: 978-681-4949
www.glcac.org/consumer.htm

Middlesex Community College
Law Center
33 Kearney Square
Lowell, MA 01852
978-656-3342
Fax: 978-441-1794
www.geocities.com/mcclawcenter

Medford Consumer Advisory
Commission
90 Main Street
Medford, MA 02155
781-393-2460
Fax: 781-393-2342

Consumer Assistance Office—
Metro West, Inc.
209 West Central Street
Natick, MA 01760
508-651-8812
Fax: 508-647-0661
www.consumermetrowest.org

Newton-Brookline Consumer
Office
Newton City Hall
1000 Commonwealth Avenue
Newton, MA 02459
617-796-1292
Fax: 617-796-1293

Mass PIRG Consumer Action
Center
182 Green Street
North Weymouth, MA 02191
781-335-0280
Fax: 781-340-3991

South Shore Community Action
Council, Inc.
265 South Meadow Road
Plymouth, MA 02360
508-747-7575 ext 226
Fax: 508-746-5140

Revere Consumer Affairs Office
150 Beach Street
Revere, MA 02151
781-286-8114
Fax: 781-485-2788

Mayor's Office of Consumer
Information
1600 East Columbus Avenue
Springfield, MA 01103
413-787-6437
Fax: 413-787-7781
www.cityofboston.gov/
consumeraffairs

Brockton residents contact:
Bentley Consumer Action Line
Lindsay Hall
Bentley College
175 Forest Street
Waltham, MA 02452
800-273-9494
Fax: 781-891-2478

Michigan

Consumer Protection Division
Office of Attorney General
P.O. Box 30213
Lansing, MI 48909
517-373-1140
877-765-8388
Fax: 517-241-3771
www.michigan.gov/ag

Macomb County Consumer
Protection Department
Office of the Prosecuting Attorney
Macomb County Administration
Building
One South Main Street
3rd Floor
Mt. Clemens, MI 48043
586-469-5350
Fax: 586-469-5609

Minnesota

Consumer Services Division
Attorney General's Office
1400 Bremer Tower
445 Minnesota Street
St. Paul, MN 55101
612-296-3353
800-657-3787
Fax: 612-282-2155
www.ag.state.mn.us/consumer

City Offices
Division of Licenses & Consumer
Services
Minneapolis Department of
Regulatory Services
City Hall
Room 1C
350 South 5th Street
Minneapolis, MN 55415
612-673-2080
612-673-2157 (TTY)
Fax: 612-673-3399
www.ci.minneapolis.mn.us

Mississippi

Consumer Protection Division
Attorney General's Office
P.O. Box 22947
Jackson, MS 39225
601-359-4230
800-281-4418
Fax: 601-359-4231
www.ago.state.ms.us

Bureau of Regulatory Services
P.O. Box 1609
Jackson, MS 39201
601-359-1148
Fax: 601-359-1175
www.mdac.state.ms.us

Missouri

Missouri Attorney General's Office
Supreme Court Building
207 West High Street
P.O. Box 899
Jefferson City, MO 65102
573-751-3321
800-392-8222
Fax: 573-751-0774
www.ago.mo.gov

Montana

Office of Consumer Protection
Department of Justice
1219 8ᵗʰ Avenue
P.O. Box 200151
Helena, MT 59620
406-444-4500
800-481-6896
Fax: 406-444-9680
www.doj.mt.gov/consumer

Nebraska

Office of the Attorney General
2115 State Capitol
Lincoln, NE 68509
402-471-2682
800-727-6432
www.ago.state.ne.us

Nevada

Southern Nevada
Consumer Affairs Division
1850 East Sahara Avenue
Suite 101
Las Vegas, NV 89104
702-486-7355
800-326-5202
Fax: 702-486-7371
www.fyiconsumer.org

Bureau of Consumer Protection
555 E. Washington Avenue
Suite 3900
Las Vegas, NV 89101
702-486-3420

Northern Nevada
Consumer Affairs Division
4600 Kietzke Lane
Building B
Suite 113
Reno, NV 89502
775-688-1800
800-326-5202
Fax: 775-688-1803
www.fyiconsumer.org

New Hampshire

Consumer Protection and
Antitrust Bureau
New Hampshire Department of
Justice
33 Capitol Street
Concord, NH 03301
603-271-3658
800-735-2964
Fax: 603-271-2110
www.doj.nh.gov/consumer/
index.html

New Jersey

Division of Consumer Affairs
Office of the Attorney General
Department of Law and Public
Safety
124 Halsey Street
Newark, NJ 07102
973-504-6200
800-242-5846
Fax: 973-273-8035
www.state.nj.us/lps/ca/home.htm

Camden County Office of
Consumer Protection/Weights and
Measures
DiPiero Center
Lakeland Road
Blackwood, NJ 08012
856-374-6161 (Consumer
Protection)
856-374-6001 (Weights & Measures)
800-999-9045
Fax: 856-232-0748
www.camdencounty.com

Cumberland County Department
of Consumer Affairs/Weight &
Measures
788 East Commerce Street
Bridgeton, NJ 08302
856-453-2203
Fax: 856-453-2206

Cape May County Consumer Affairs
Weights and Measures
4 Moore Road DN 310\302
Cape May Court House, NJ 08210
609-463-6475
Fax: 609-463-6472
www.capemaycountygov.net

Essex County Division of
CommunityAction/Consumer
Services
50 South Clinton Street
Suite 3201
East Orange, NJ 07018
973-395-8350
Fax: 973-395-8433

Hunterdon County Office of
Consumer Affairs
P.O. Box 2900
Flemington, NJ 08822
908-806-5174
Fax: 908-806-2057

Monmouth County Department of
Consumer Affairs
50 East Main Street
P.O. Box 1255
Freehold, NJ 07728
732-431-7900
Fax: 732-845-2037

Bergen County Office of Consumer
Protection
One Bergen County Plaza
3rd Floor
Hackensack, NJ 07601-7000
201-336-6400
Fax: 201-336-6414

Hudson County Division of
Consumer Affairs
583 Newark Avenue
Jersey City, NJ 07306
201-795-6295
201-795-6163
Fax: 201-795-6468

Burlington County Office of
Consumer Affairs/Weights and
Measures
49 Rancocas Road
P.O. Box 6000
Mount Holly, NJ 08060
609-265-5098 (Weights & Measures)
609-265-5054 (Consumer Affairs)
Fax: 609-265-5065

Middlesex County Consumer
Affairs
Middlesex County Administration
Building
JFK Square
2nd Floor, Suite 290
New Brunswick, NJ 08901
732-745-3875
Fax: 732-745-3815
www.co.midddlesex.nj.us

Somerset County Division of
Consumer Affairs
P.O. Box 3000
Somerville, NJ 08876
908-203-6080
Fax: 908-575-3905

Ocean County Department of
Consumer Affairs/Weights and
Measures
1027 Hooper Avenue
P.O. Box 2191
Toms River, NJ 08754-2191
732-929-2105
800-722-0291 ext. 2105
Fax: 732-506-5330

Passaic County Department of
Consumer Protection/Weights and
Measures
Department of Law
1310 Route 23 North
Wayne, NJ 07470
973-305-5750 (Weights & Measures)
973-305-5881 (Consumer
Protection)
Fax: 973-628-1796

Union County Division of
Consumer Affairs
300 North Avenue East
Westfield, NJ 07090
908-654-9840
Fax: 908-654-3082
www.unioncountynj.org

Gloucester County Department of
Consumer Protection
Weights and Measures
115 Budd Boulevard
Woodbury, NJ 08096
856-384-6855
856-848-6616 (TDD)
Fax: 856-384-6858
www.co.gloucester.nj.us/
protection

City Offices
1200 Mountain Avenue
Middlesex, NJ 08846
732-356-8090 ext. 250
Fax: 732-356-1249

Nutley Consumer Affairs
Public Affairs Building
149 Chestnut Street
Nutley, NJ 07110
973-284-4975
Fax: 973-661-9411

Perth Amboy Consumer Affairs
Office of Social Services
Fayette and Read Streets
Perth Amboy, NJ 08861
732-826-4300
Fax: 732-826-6192

Plainfield Action Services
City Hall Annex
510 Watchung Avenue
Plainfield, NJ 07060
908-753-3519
Fax: 908-753-3540

Secaucus Department of Consumer
Affairs
Municipal Government Center
1203 Patterson Plank Road
Secaucus, NJ 07094
201-330-2008

Consumer Affairs Office
1976 Morris Avenue
Union, NJ 07083
908-851-5477
Fax: 908-851-4679

Woodbridge Township Consumer
Affairs
Municipal Building
One Main Street
Woodbridge, NJ 07095
732-634-4500
Fax: 732-602-6016

New Mexico
Consumer Protection Division
P.O. Drawer 1508
Santa Fe, NM 87504
505-827-6000
800-678-1508
Fax: 505-827-5826
www.ago.state.nm.us

New York
Bureau of Consumer Frauds and
Protection
Office of the Attorney General
State Capitol
Albany, NY 12224
518-474-7330
800-771-7755
www.oag.state.ny.us

New York State Consumer
Protection Board
5 Empire State Plaza
Suite 2101
Albany, NY 12223
518-474-8583
800-697-1220
Fax: 518-486-3936
E-mail:
www.nysconsumer.gov

Consumer Frauds and Protection Bureau
Office of the Attorney General
120 Broadway
3rd Floor
New York, NY 10271
212-416-8000
212-416-8345
800-771-7755
800-788-9898
212-416-8893
Fax: 212-416-6003

Regional Offices
Binghamton Regional Office
Office of the Attorney General
State Office Building
17th Floor
44 Hawley Street
Binghamton, NY 13901
607-721-8771

Hauppauge Regional Office
Office of the Attorney General
300 Motor Parkway
Suite 205
Hauppauge, NY 11788
516-231-2400

Minneola Regional Office
Office of the Attorney General
200 Old Country Road
New York, NY 11501
516-248-3302

Harlem Regional Office
Office of the Attorney General
163 West 125th Street
New York, NY 10027-8201
212-961-4475
Fax: 212-961-4003

Plattsburgh Regional Office
Office of the Attorney General
70 Clinton Street
Plattsburgh, NY 12901-2818
518-562-3282

Rochester Regional Office
Office of the Attorney General
144 Exchange Boulevard
Rochester, NY 14614
585-546-7430

Utica Regional Office
Office of the Attorney General
207 Genesee Street
Room 508
Utica, NY 13501
315-793-2225
Fax: 315-793-2228

Watertown Regional Office
Office of the Attorney General
Dulles State Office Building
317 Washington Street
Watertown, NY 13601
315-785-2444

Westchester Regional Office
Office of the Attorney General
101 East Post Road
White Plains, NY 10601
914-422-8755
Fax: 914-422-8706

County Offices
Department of Consumer
Affairs/Weights & Measures
112 State Street
Room 1207
Albany, NY 12207
518-447-7581
Fax: 518-487-5048
www.albanycounty.com

Consumer Fraud Bureau
Erie County District Attorney's
Office
Statler Towers
107 Delaware Avenue
4th Floor
Buffalo, NY 14202
716-853-8404
800-771-7755
Fax: 716-853-8414

Putnam County Department of
Consumer Affairs/Weights and
Measures
110 Old Route 6
Building 3
Carmel, NY 10512
845-225-2039
Fax: 845-225-3403

Orange County Department of
Consumer Affairs and Weights
and Measures
99 Main Street
Goshen, NY 10924
845-291-2400
Fax: 845-291-2385

Ulster County District Attorney's
Consumer Fraud Bureau
20 Lucas Avenue
Kingston, NY 12401
845-340-3260

Nassau County Office of Consumer
Affairs
200 County Seat Drive
Mineola, NY 11501
516-571-2600

Sullivan County Department of
Consumer Affairs
Sullivan County Government
Center
100 North Street
P.O. Box 5012
Monticello, NY 12701
845-794-3000
Fax: 845-794-0230

Rockland County Office of
Consumer Protection
18 New Hempstead Road
6th Floor
New City, NY 10956
845-708-7600
Fax: 845-708-7616

Dutchess County Department of
Consumer Affairs
98 Peach Road
Poughkeepsie, NY 12601
845-486-2949
Fax: 845-486-2947
www.dutchessny.gov

Schenectady County Consumer
Affairs
64 Kellar Avenue
Schenectady, NY 12307
518-356-6795
518-356-7473
Fax: 518-357-0319

Westchester County District
Attorney's Office
Economic Crimes Unit
County Courthouse
111 Martin Luther King Jr.
Boulevard
White Plains, NY 10601
914-995-3303
Fax: 914-995-3594

Westchester County Department
of Consumer Protection
112 East Post Road
4th Floor
White Plains, NY 10601
914-995-2155
Fax: 914-995-3115

City Offices
Mt. Vernon Office of Consumer
Protection/Bureau of Weights and
Measures
1 Roosevelt Square
Room 11
Mount Vernon, NY 10550
914-665-2433

New York City Department of
Consumer Affairs
42 Broadway
New York, NY 10004
212-487-4444
212-487-4465 (TDD)
www.ci.nyc.ny.us/html/dca/
home.html

Town of Colonia Consumer
Protection
Memorial Town Hall
Newtonville, NY 12128
518-783-2790

Schenectady Bureau of Consumer
Protection
City Hall
Room 204
Jay Street
Schenectady, NY 12305
518-382-5061
Fax: 518-382-5074

Yonkers Office of Consumer
Protection
87 Nepperhan Avenue
Yonkers, NY 10701
914-377-6808
Fax: 914-377-6811

North Carolina
Consumer Protection Division
Office of the Attorney General
9001 Mail Service Center
Raleigh, NC 27699
919-716-6400
877-566-7226
www.ncdoj.com

North Dakota
Consumer Protection and Antitrust
Division
Office of the Attorney General
State Capitol
600 East Boulevard Avenue
Department 125
Bismarck, ND 58502
701-328-3404
800-472-2600
www.ag.state.nd.us

Ohio
Consumer Protection Section
Attorney General's Office
30 East Broad Street
17th Floor
Columbus, OH 43215
614-466-1305
614-466-4320
www.ag.state.oh.us

Ohio Consumers' Counsel
10 West Broad Street
Suite 1800
Columbus, OH 43215
614-466-8574
877-742-5622
www.pickocc.org

County Offices
P.O. Box 22448
Akron, OH 44302
330-643-2879
www.co.summit.oh.us/
conaffairs.htm

Oklahoma

Commission on Consumer Credit
4545 North Lincoln Boulevard
Suite 104
Oklahoma City, OK 73105
405-521-3653
800-448-4904
Fax: 405-521-6740
www.okdocc.state.ok.us

Consumer Protection Unit
Oklahoma Attorney General
2300 North Lincoln Boulevard
Suite 112
Oklahoma City, OK 73105
405-521-3921
Fax: 405-522-4534
www.oag.state.ok.us

Oregon

Consumer Protection Section
Department of Justice
1162 Court Street NE
Salem, OR 97301
503-378-4320
503-229-5576
877-877-9392
Fax: 503-378-5017
www.doj.state.or.us

Pennsylvania

Office of the Attorney General
Bureau of Consumer Protection
14th Floor
Strawberry Square
Harrisburg, PA 17120
717-787-9707
800-441-2555
Fax: 717-787-1190
www.attorneygeneral.gov

Office of the Consumer Advocate
Office of the Attorney General
Forum Place
5th Floor
Harrisburg, PA 17101
717-783-5048
800-684-6560
Fax: 717-783-7152
www.oca.state.pa.us

Regional Offices
Office of the Attorney General
801 Hamilton Street
4th Floor
Allentown, PA 18101
610-821-6690
Fax: 610-821-6529

Ebensburg Regional Office—
Bureau of Consumer Protection
Office of the Attorney General
171 Lovell Avenue
Suite 202
Ebensburg, PA 15931
814-471-1831
Fax: 814-471-1840

Erie Regional Office—Bureau of
Consumer Protection
Office of the Attorney General
1001 State Street
Suite 1009
Erie, PA 16501
814-871-4371
Fax: 814-871-4848

Harrisburg Regional Office—
Bureau of Consumer Protection
Office of the Attorney General
301 Chestnut Street
Suite 105
Harrisburg, PA 17101
717-787-7109
Fax: 717-772-3560

Scranton Regional Office—Bureau
of Consumer Protection
Office of the Attorney General
100 Samter Building
101 Penn Avenue
Scranton, PA 18503
570-963-4913
Fax: 570-963-3418

County Offices
Bucks County Consumer
Protection, Weights and Measures
50 North Main Street
Doylestown, PA 18901
215-348-7442
Fax: 215-348-4570

Delaware County Consumer
Affairs
Delaware County Courthouse
201 West Front Street
Media, PA 19063
610-891-4865
Fax: 610-566-3947

Montgomery County Consumer
Affairs
Montgomery County Human
Services Center
1430 DeKalb Street
P.O. Box 311
Norristown, PA 19404
610-278-3565
Fax: 610-278-5228
www.montcopa.org/
consumeraffairs

Chester County Consumer Affairs
601 Westtown Road
Suite 295
West Chester, PA 19382
610-344-6150
www.chesco.org/health/
consaffairs

Puerto Rico
Department of Justice
P.O. Box 920192
San Juan, PR 00902
787-721-2900
Fax: 787-724-6880
www.justica.govierno.pr

Rhode Island
Consumer Protection Unit
Department of the Attorney General
150 South Main Street
Providence, RI 02903
401-274-4400 x2359
Fax: 401-222-2725
www.riag.state.ri.us

South Carolina
South Carolina Department of
Consumer Affairs
3600 Forest Drive
3rd Floor
P.O. Box 5757
Columbia, SC 29250
803-734-4200
800-922-1594
Fax: 803-734-4286
www.scconsumer.gov

Office of the Attorney General
P.O. Box 11549
Columbia, SC 29211
803-734-3970
Fax: 803-734-4323
www.scattorneygeneral.org

State Ombudsman
Office of Executive Policy and
Program
1205 Pendleton Street
Room 308
Columbia, SC 29201
803-734-5049
866-300-9333
Fax: 803-734-0799
www.myscgov.com

South Dakota
Division of Consumer Protection
Office of the Attorney General
1302 East Highway 14
Pierre, SD 57501
605-773-4400
800-300-1986
Fax: 605-773-7163
www.state.sd.us/atg

Tennessee
Consumer Affairs
500 James Robertson Parkway
Nashville, TN 37243
615-741-4737
800-342-8385
Fax: 615-532-4994
www.state.tn.us/consumer

Consumer Advocate and
Protection Division
Office of the Attorney General
P.O. Box 20207
Nashville, TN 37202
615-741-1671
www.attorneygeneral.state.tn.us

Texas
Office of the Attorney General
Consumer Protection
300 West 15th Street
9th Floor
P.O. Box 12548
Austin, TX 78711
512-463-2185
800-621-0508
Fax: 512-473-8301
www.oag.state.tx.us

County Offices
District Attorney's Office
1201 Franklin
Suite 600
Houston, TX 77002
713-755-5836
Fax: 713-755-5262

City Offices
Department of Environmental and
Health Services
City Hall
Room 7A-North
1500 Marilla
Dallas, TX 75201
214-670-5711
Fax: 214-670-3863

Utah
Division of Consumer Protection
Department of Commerce
160 East 300 South
Box 146704
Salt Lake City, UT 84114
801-530-6601
Fax: 801-530-6001
800-721-7233
www.consumerprotection.utah.gov

Vermont
Consumer Assistance Program
Office of the Attorney General
206 Morrill Hall, UVM
Burlington, VT 05405
802-656-3183
800-649-2424
Fax: 802-656-1423
www.atg.state.vt.us

Office of the Attorney General
Consumer Protection Unit
109 State Street
Montpelier, VT 05609
802-828-5507
Fax: 802-828-2154

Virgin Islands
Department of Licensing and
Consumer Affairs
Golden Rock Shopping Center
Christiansted
St. Croix, VI 00820
340-773-2226
Fax: 340-778-8250
www.dlca.gov.vi

Property and Procurement
Building
No. 1 Sub Base
Room 205
St. Thomas, VI 00802
340-774-3130
Fax: 340-776-0675
www.dlca.gov.vi

Virginia
Consumer Assistance
Office of the Attorney General
900 East Main Street
Richmond, VA 23219
804-786-2071
Fax: 804-786-0122
www.oag.state.va.us

Virginia Department of Agriculture
and Consumer Services
Consumer Affairs
102 Governor Street
Richmond, VA 23219
804-786-2042
800-552-9963
Fax: 804-225-7479
www.vdacs.state.va.us

County Offices
Consumer Affairs Office
One Court House Plaza
Suite 302
2100 Clarendon Boulevard
Arlington, VA 22201
703-228-3260
Fax: 703-228-3295
www.arlingtonva.us

Fairfax County Department of
Cable Communications and
Consumer Protection
12000 Government Center
Parkway
Suite 433
Fairfax, VA 22035
703-222-8435
703-324-8484
Fax: 703-322-9542

City Offices
Consumer Affairs
City Hall
P.O. Box 178
Alexandria, VA 22313
703-838-4350
703-838-5056 (TDD)
Fax: 703-838-6426
www.alexandria.va.gov

Office of the Commonwealth's
Attorney
Consumer Affairs Division
2425 Nimmo Parkway
Virginia Beach, VA 23456
757-426-5836
Fax: 757-427-8779
www.vbgov.com/dept/oca/ca.htm

Washington
Office of the Attorney General
1125 Washington Street SE
Olympia, WA 98504
360-753-6200
800-551-4636
www.atg.wa.gov

Regional Offices
Office of the Attorney General
103 East Holly Street
Suite 308
Bellingham, WA 98225
360-738-6185
800-551-4636
Fax: 360-738-6190
www.atg.wa.gov

Kennewick Consumer Resource
Center (Southeast Washington)
Office of the Attorney General
500 North Morain Street
Suite 1250
Kennewick, WA 99336
509-734-7140
800-551-4636
Fax: 509-734-7475
www.atg.wa.gov

Vancouver Consumer Resource
Center (Southwest Washington)
Office of the Attorney General
1220 Main Street
Suite 549
Vancouver, WA 98660
360-759-2150
800-551-4636
Fax: 360-759-2159
www.atg.wa.gov

West Virginia

Consumer Protection Division
Office of the Attorney General
P.O. Box 1789
Charleston, WV 25326
304-558-8986
800-368-8808
www.wvago.us

Wisconsin

Department of Agriculture, Trade
and Consumer Protection
P.O. Box 8911
Madison, WI 53708
608-224-4949
800-422-7128
Fax: 608-224-4939
www.datcp.state.wi.us

Regional Offices
Department of Agriculture, Trade
and Consumer Protection
200 North Jefferson Street
Suite 146A
Green Bay, WI 54301
920-448-5110
Fax: 920-448-5118

Bureau of Consumer Protection
Department of Agriculture, Trade
and Consumer Protection
10930 West Potter Road
Suite C
Milwaukee, WI 53226
414-266-1231

County Offices
717 Wisconsin Avenue
Racine, WI 53403
262-636-3126
Fax: 262-637-5279

Wyoming
Consumer Protection Unit
123 State Capitol
Cheyenne, WY 82002
307-777-7874
800-438-5799
Fax: 307-777-7956

Appendix B

Federal Trade Commision Regional Offices

States in Region	Office and Addresses
Alabama, Florida, Georgia Mississippi, North Carolina South Carolina, Tennessee	Southeast Region 225 Peachtree Street Suite 1500 Atlanta, GA 30303 877-382-4357
Connecticut, Maine, Massachusetts, New Hampshire, Rhode Island, Vermont, New Jersey	Northeast Region 1 Bowling Green New York, NY 10004 877-382-4357
Illinois, Indiana, Iowa, Kentucky Minnesota, Missouri, Wisconsin, Kansas, Nebraska, North & South, Dakota	55 East Monroe Street Suite 1860 Chicago, IL 60603 877-382-4357
Michigan, Ohio, Pennsylvania West Virginia, Delaware, Maryland, Virginia, Washington, DC	1111 Superior Avenue Suite 200 Cleveland, OH 44114 877-382-4357

States in Region	Office and Addresses
Arkansas, Louisiana, New Mexico Oklahoma, Texas	1999 Bryan Street Suite 2150 Dallas, TX 75201 877-382-4357
Arizona, California, Colorado, Hawaii, Nevada, Utah	901 Market Street Suite 570 San Francisco, CA 95103 877-382-4357
Alaska, Idaho, Oregon, Washington, Montana, Wyoming	10877 Wilshire Boulevard Suite 700 Los Angeles, CA 90024 877-382-4357

Appendix C

Statutes of Limitation

The *Statute of Limitations* is the law that sets the time period in which a lawsuit can be filed after a specified event. The time periods listed on the following pages are all in years. More detailed information follows the listing.

A *written contract* is one that has been signed by the parties. A *promissory note* is a document that has been signed stating the amount to be paid and the manner in which it is to be paid. The promissory note usually includes a provision for default—i.e., what the creditor or lender can do in the event payment is not made as required in the note.

As you will see in the following list, the time period in which a creditor can file a lawsuit to collect on a promissory note is generally the same as the time limitation for suing on a written contract. Only two states, Delaware and Louisiana, set a different time limitation for suing on a promissory note.

An *oral contract* is just that—a verbal agreement to do something that has not been reduced to writing and signed by the parties.

The list is by no means exhaustive. You should consult your state laws for more specific information. Typically, the reference to the Statute of Limitations can be found in the index to your state statutes, under the heading "Limitation of Actions." To get you started, following is a list of some of the statutory references, state by state. However, these include only the limitations listed above.

There may be additional and different time limitations for lawsuits on sales contracts, open-end revolving accounts, lawsuits for damages, etc.

Also, you will be able to find your state's time limitation for filing a lawsuit to collect a judgment.

NOTE: *All time periods listed refer to years.*

State	Written Contracts	Promissory Notes	Oral Contracts	Statutory Reference
Alabama	6	6	6	6-23-33, 6-2-34
Alaska	6	6	6	09.10.050, 45-02-725
Arizona	6	5	3	12-548, 12-543
Arkansas	5	6	3	16-56-115, 16-56-105
California	4	4	2	CCP 337
Colorado	6	6	6	13-80-103.5
Connecticut	6	6	3	52-576, 52-581
Delaware	3	6	3	10-8106, 10-8109
District of Col.	3	3	3	12-301
Florida	5	5	4	95.11
Georgia	6	6	4	9-3-24, 9-3-25
Hawaii	6	6	6	657-1
Idaho	5	10	4	5-216, 5-217
Illinois	10	6	5	13-206, 13-205
Indiana	10	10	6	34-1-2-1
Iowa	10	10	5	614.1
Kansas	5	5	3	60.511, 60.512
Kentucky	15	15	5	413.090, 413.120
Louisiana	10	10	10	CC 3509, 3478
Maine	6	6	6	14-751
Maryland	3	6	3	CJ 5-101
Massachusetts	6	6	6	260.2
Michigan	6	6	6	600.5813, 451.435
Minnesota	6	6	6	541.05
Mississippi	3	3	3	752-725, 15-1-29

State	Written Contracts	Promissory Notes	Oral Contracts	Statutory Reference
Missouri	10	10	5	516.110, 516.120
Montana	8	8	5	27-2-202
Nebraska	5	6	4	25-205, 25-206
Nevada	6	3	4	11.90
New Hampshire	3	6	3	508:4
New Jersey	6	6	6	2A:14-1
New Mexico	6	6	4	37-1-3, 37-1-4
New York	6	6	6	CPLR 213(2)
North Carolina	3	5	3	CP 1-52.
North Dakota	6	6	6	28-01-16
Ohio	15	15	6	2305.06, 2305.07
Oklahoma	5	5	3	12 Sec. 95
Oregon	6	6	6	12.080
Pennsylvania	6	4	4	42 Sec. 5525
Rhode Island	15	10	15	9-1-13(a)
South Carolina	10	3	10	15-3-350
South Dakota	6	6	6	15-2-13
Tennessee	6	6	6	28-3-109
Texas	4	4	4	16.004
Utah	6	6	4	28-12-23, 28-12-25
Vermont	6	5	6	12-511
Virginia	5	6	3	8.01-246
Washington	6	6	3	4.16.040, 4.16.080
West Virginia	10	6	5	55-2-6
Wisconsin	6	10	6	893.43
Wyoming	10	10	8	1-3-105

Appendix D

Frequently Referenced Laws

The *Consumer Credit Act* covers disclosure requirements for most credit transactions, credit reporting agencies, and collection agencies. (U.S.C., Title 15, Chapter 41.) The Act now includes the following laws that are referenced in this book:

- Consumer Credit Cost Disclosure (Truth in Lending), U.S.C., Title 15, Chapter 41, Section 1601 and the Truth-in-Lending regulations (Regulation Z), Code of Federal Regulations Title 12, Part 226, ensuring that everyone who has a need for consumer credit is given meaningful information regarding the cost of the credit.

United States Code, Title 15, Chapter 41 includes the following.

- Fair Credit Billing Act (regulating the manner in which you are billed by creditors and the information that must be disclosed to you).
- Consumer Leasing Act of 1976.
- Credit advertising. (See Truth in Lending Regulations Appendices for sample calculations and disclosure form.)
- Restrictions on garnishment are set forth in U.S.C., Title 15, Section 1667, Title III.
- Fair Debt Collection Practices Act, U.S.C., Title 15, Section 1692, Public Law 95-109 (regulating the practices of collection agencies).

- Consumer Credit Reporting Act of 1996, U.S.C., Title 15, Section 1601, Public Law 104-208 (regulating the practices of credit reporting agencies or credit bureaus).
- U.S.C., Title 11, U.S. Bankruptcy Code generally.
- U.S.C., Title 11, Chapter 7, Liquidation.
- U.S.C., Title 11, Chapter 13, Adjustment of Debts of an Individual with Regular Income (Wage Earner Plan).
- U.S.C., Title 29, Internal Revenue Code generally.
- U.S.C., Title 29, Section 6334, Internal Revenue Exemptions.

Index

About the Author

Gudrun Maria Nickel has degrees from the University of Kansas, University of Wisconsin in Milwaukee, and Washburn University School of Law in Topeka, Kansas. She is licensed to practice law in Florida, Montana, Illinois, and Kansas. In addition to maintaining a full-time law office, Ms. Nickel has authored books on a variety of subjects, including debtor and creditor rights, Florida probate, guardianship, and adoptions. She also authored a book in the German language about U.S. immigration issues.

During the past twenty years she has served on the board of directors of her area's Consumer Credit Counseling Services agency, provided pro-bono credit consulting services to clients of a local governmental extension office, assisted in bankruptcy filings, handled foreclosures, and represented creditors and debtors in debt collection cases.

To discuss debt and credit issues—particularly as outlined in her previous book *Debtors' Rights*, Ms. Nickel also appeared on national television programs including *CNN*, Lifetime channel's *New Attitudes*, and MSNBC, as well as numerous radio programs.